'Doing' Church

K B Napier

'Doing' Church

K B Napier

ISBN No. 978-1-716-05417-4

Petra Press, PO Box 415, SA5 8YH   UK

Contents

A Look Back

When my family, friends, and I left what we call the 'system' of traditional churches, many wondered what on earth I was doing. Most thought I was backsliding, even without talking to me or pondering on what was happening. I was even accused of wrongfully taking members from the traditionalist church we all attended. In fact, everyone else left first, and I reluctantly left last – an urban legend bites the dust! But, this is now irrelevant and people choose what they wish to believe.

The book looks at why the traditional church is unbiblical, and why my website is sub-titled 'Reformed and Reforming'. Our spiritual lives are thus dynamic and keep moving forward, with many obstacles along the way. The reader will observe that I have little regard for traditionalist churches, but this does not mean I have no regard for those caught in their web. Of necessity the book is tough-talking.

In this book I include some of the material found in the much shorter book, 'Will The Real Pastor Please Stand Up?' plus more, such as ideas from 'Patchwork Quilt Theology', and 'The Left Boot of Fellowship'. I hope to show that what Christians mean by 'doing church' is very much off the mark, and their thinking is far removed from what God requires of us. (Even the phrase itself - 'doing church' - shows a wrong attitude). Who am I to talk like this? I am nobody. But, I do read scripture and allow it to interpret itself. I KNOW I am right about my criticism, because I was once caught by the same traditionalism for twenty years. My words are for your consideration, and not for self-satisfaction. I will begin in the late 1970s…

A Surprise Request

During a meeting in the church I attended, my then pastor took me aside and asked "Will you pastor your own family?" He gave no explanation. At that time (being saved over ten years earlier in 1965) I was, like almost every other traditional Christian, of the opinion that the pastor was the boss, to be revered and followed, no matter what. I was puzzled by his request, but accepted. (I had been doing that anyway, because family tended to seek my views).

My family and extended family is large, and at that time I was working in a psychiatric hospital where I was literally forced to defend my faith every day, sometimes against much scorn and challenges. I was also teaching a weekly Bible study for family and a few friends, including a distant cousin who was training to be a Church in Wales priest.

I lived in a small council house, with just a kitchen and lounge downstairs – so not much room. My kitchen table was perpetually strewn with commentaries and other biblical aids and the Greek alphabet and words covered the walls, written on paper sheets.

My dear wife, Diane, did not complain and was always encouraging. On top of that I usually preached in a variety of churches most Sundays and some weekdays, in Wales and England. I never accepted money for this, not even for expenses. During my 'traditional' time, covering a span of 20 years, I was offered three or four paid pastorates, which I refused. (Though the calls were genuine, I did not have the assurance of the Holy Spirit to enable me to accept).

The meetings had gone on for several years before the pastor made his request. I was already used to answering queries from those who attended. Most of my counsel was given whilst working in the hospital. Every day a patient or staff member asked me for advice or my Christian answer to this or that problem or issue. So, pastoring my family was just an extension of what I was already doing.

The 'twenty year itch'
However, as I have mentioned elsewhere many times, this only continued for about twenty years after I was saved (I used to think it was just ten years but a recent rethink shows twice that time elapsed). In the latter part of those years I began to question myself and what I was doing. Something wasn't right but I did not know what.

As I admitted to one man of my own age, "I feel like I am a bear tied to a post and can't break free. I feel taunted but cannot do anything". (That same man is now retired but he still tries to avoid me, for reasons that are unknown to me).

I also made the mistake of saying perhaps I ought to begin a ministry to deal with the odd problem areas that were pressed into my heart. This wasn't a personal choice, but a vague realization that something needed to be done: my soul was being distressed but I had no idea why. The look of disapproval on his face was priceless and he said that I couldn't possibly do that without the pastor's and elders' approval.

But, my mind was troubled and the idea was always there; I didn't generate it, it was simply there, like a thorn. And, I knew that my 'betters' would not approve, no matter what I said. So, 'something isn't right' haunted my mind for years and no-one was able to point me in the right direction. I was hovering on the edge of a big change, one that I knew would not delight my hierarchical leaders. So, I remained a drone, a copy of my peers.

Then (again I have spoken of this moment several times), as I studied Samuel, the whole problem dissolved and yet 'hotted up'. It only took one small verse to sort my mind out. From that very small source came an entirely new spiritual life. It was the point at which all my doubts and queries exploded, taking me away from tradition and into an amazing world of God's will and true freedom in Christ. Sadly, many were afraid to talk to me about it, so I had no 'sounding board' to bounce my thoughts off. I only knew that something different was coming.

Frankly it scared me, but it was also exciting. That single Bible verse was the catalyst used by God to show me the reality of being a believer. But, just as Job was accused of so many sins he had not committed, so my fellows accused me of backsliding. Or, they (the people who once knew me as a fellow member) simply stopped talking to me! This is still what happens, more than 35 years later.

This book, then, is about our journey from traditionalism to authentic beliefs, free of the hampering and dampening effect of unbiblical thoughts. Though anecdotal, it is also biblical. I have included our Publications' List, because many of our thoughts are contained in the articles shown, and in the Bible commentaries and studies. It is how we moved from false faith to genuine reality. It is up to the reader to use it as he or she wishes. I feel sadness that so many true believers are unable to break free from traditionalism.

Unthinking Christians
In any activity we can find this stark hatred, or maybe fear, when someone stands out from the crowd and refuses to be propagandized. Today, as I write, the false Covid virus narrative is pushed down everyone's throats. Socialism is being forced on us by governments. 'Green' fake environmentalism is doing the same (see my large book, 'Global Green

Agenda', 2009). And the iron fist of Islam is being portrayed as 'good' so that western people will accept Muslim domination without argument.

From what I can see, the same process is happening within the churches: many Christians do not think and just accept whatever is thrust into their minds by the unsaved, and even by saved people who prefer tradition to truth. This causes me intense concern, that Christians do not even bother to think properly, and they have no critical sense (or, more precisely, they cannot be bothered to use it, though God has given them the ability), so are easily led by popular figures and fashionable magazine articles.

As soon as I discovered my gross errors in being 'traditional'*, changes hit me head-on! In my first 20 years I was 'accepted' (though I now doubt it was genuine), but the moment I stepped away from the hallowed path of traditionalism I was not allowed a voice and was quickly avoided if not shunned. Therefore, no-one heard my reasons for leaving tradition behind. They just assumed I had somehow 'gone bad'. Which, in itself, proves that previous 'friendships' could be questioned… surely, if I really HAD become 'rogue', someone would have come to my side and counselled me? Or, attempt to find out what was going on? But, no-one did. And after a while I could see God's hand in all of it. (*there are two kinds of 'tradition' – good or bad, 'traditionalism'; in this book I refer to the bad, which is almost universally practiced).

Preach Truth – Stop Preaching!

From that juncture in my life, preaching invites stopped. It was amazing how the jungle telegraph spread the news! This is because I no longer tried to preach according to the 'Geneva Pulpit' technique! Also, I realized how foolish I had been, trying to copy my peer preachers! Instead, I preached truth undiluted. And, in turn, I did not wish to preach in churches that did not want truth.

I had the strong impression that days of honest preaching were gone anyway, because genuine preaching did not fulfill traditionalist views and wishes. Thus, I did not take up invitations to pastor churches, one in my home town, and three in England. I also had to step back from my appointment as head of a ministry that was also attached to pastoring a large church, in the east of England. (I had actually moved to the location after being appointed, but God led me out again).

Quite soon after all this I had to come away totally. Strangely, it was family and friends who left the 'system' first. Then, as I hung on, a good friend and pastor, Dr Peter Trumper, called me and advised that I should follow God's plan for me and leave; he encouraged me in my new publishing ministry. So I did. His counsel was repeated by a local pastor, Arthur Harris, who was well thought of in church circles. So they could avoid being interrogated about me, I never mentioned their friendship to others.

In the first week of leaving our final traditionalist church, the call from God was poured out upon my life like a flood, and confirmation came from unsought biblical texts, and by assurances from our new church. For reasons I did not know at the time, they all unanimously said I was now their pastor. Frankly, I did not choose the role, but everything moved in that direction. At that time there were well over 20 souls, plus children. I offer my opinion, that when God calls a man to pastorship, it is surrounded by proofs and many 'incidents' that lead a man in that direction. It is not a simple step of "Let's do it" out of the blue!

Plan of Action – Do Nothing
The very first task was for us to do nothing. We decided to test absolutely everything by seeking the help of the Holy Spirit, scripture, and God's assurances. Every part of what we had done in the 'system' was tested deeply, and out of that came our doctrinal beliefs (which are fully scriptural). While we were examining everything, we did not have the usual Bible studies – and 'sermons' were definitely out as useless encumbrances!

The basics took three years to come to life as we structured our fellowship as God demanded – we left traditionalist approaches far behind. (Note: In this book, I use 'tradition' and 'traditionalist' as equal terms. We acknowledge that some traditions are acceptable and biblical). At times we scared ourselves by ditching traditional beliefs in favour of what scripture plainly told us. And much of it was portrayed in the first articles published by me. My brother-in-Law James, was led to assist technically, something that has proved to be vital; without his work I could not do mine). Initially, this was shared by two others, African PhD university students (one of whom now has a flourishing ministry in his own country). The 'structure' quickly slimmed down.

The ministry started out for university students and lecturers, but very quickly God changed this to a wider general 'audience', much as we have it today. At first we were named 'Christian Research Institute', but this was altered when we realized many who saw the title thought we were a 'red brick' college, and, there was already a group with the same name in the USA. Hence, we became the ministry as we have it today: Bible Theology Ministries (BTM), which more accurately describes what we do. Over a short time, several who had helped us, including in Singapore, went their ways… it was simply how God organised everything!

The ministry was fronted by a 'CRI Pack' containing a mini-newspaper plus several separate articles. It was quarterly at that time because that is how long it took to produce each Pack. We had no computers, so the 'old' ways were used. Images had to be personally drawn, then cut out and pasted onto sheets. The same happened with reports etc. I had to type out the material. James then took it to his university department secretary, who retyped on a professional electronic typewriter. The text was then cut and pasted onto fresh sheets, collated, and then photocopied ready to send out. It was very hard work! The coming of computers led to very fast production, storage and printing!

No Need for Expense
During this start-up period, I was myself a 'mature' student, and still pastored and taught our own church. This was held in our homes (finally established in my own home for a variety of reasons). There was no good reason to hire a hall or buy a property. Then, we numbered over 20 persons (more than you find in many traditional churches), not including visitors or children.

At times the Sunday meetings were bursting at the seams, and sometimes people had to sit on stairs and in the corridor close to the main room. But, we managed. Then and now I received no income from any of these activities. We toyed with this at one time but it was not from God so we put it aside.

Frankly, I am glad today that we also stopped asking for a subscription fee for our printed materials (CRI Packs). We decided that if God would carry us forward without us seeking money, then all the better. Or, to put it another way, I said that when all helps stopped, it would signal the cessation of my ministry. Nowadays almost all such 'helps' are from myself, or James! At times we struggle, but God makes sure we continue, such is the vital need.

Since stopping subscription fees we continued to work in a small way compared to the 'big' ministries that DO seek money. And I have never been given a salary for pastoring our church. This proved to be for our good, for ministries and churches that rely on asking people for money are very prone to disaster and closing down. They focus more on obtaining cash than on any ministry they claim to have.

We also rejected the idea of making ourselves into a charity. Being a charity would have brought much income, but it would mean agreeing to governmental interference and demands. Too many charities have to adjust their aims and wordage to suit the demands of sexual perversion laws. We prefer having little or no money to obeying government's illicit or godless dictates. Thus, we (James and I) have always paid for what we do out of our own pockets, hard though it can be and often is.

We were, in fact, following biblical patterns, even by meeting in our homes. It is where the early churches met. Some continued to attend synagogues, but did not follow Judaism. However, this did not last long, and rabbis politely asked Christians to leave. But, then, along came the cementing of traditional 'Christianity' into a fixed form. as Roman Christians turned to an Old Testament-style liturgical form.

Today, this form, Roman Catholicism, is very influential, a heresy of the highest order. It is supported by its sister heretical 'church',

Anglicanism. Crushed in between are the 'Protestant' churches, who themselves crush independent local churches like ours. But, it doesn't work – God has other plans!

When I was saved it was after spending the previous 18 years in and around churches. During that time I had no idea about scripture and biblical truth though I heard it all the time. For me it was just a social thing. But, almost as soon as I was saved I began to have doubts about what I was saying and doing, and what I heard; I could not match what I was being taught with what scripture said! The same problem stayed with me, and remains with me to this day. The 'something' that was wrong is traditionalism, and nearly all local churches are subject to traditionalism rather than to pure scripture.

It is the subject of this book, because millions of Christians suppress the truth by adhering to traditions that are useless. Just about all churches today copy Romanistic ecclesiology, even if in minor ways. This harms the people of God as well as the Name of God. Others (such as rampant charismatics) go the other way and cast-off the older traditions, only to make up their own. This is just as harmful to spiritual life!

The early churches knew nothing of total rule by pastors, supported by 'elders' and 'deacons'. The roles are certainly found in scripture – but not as we know them today. Nor did they know anything about 'sermons', rigid scheduled prayer meetings, or many of the traditions we have now. In the earliest days 'worship' meetings like those we see today were unknown. Everything was fluid, and depended solely on how a meeting was led by the Holy Spirit, Who prompted those present to speak, or sing. Meetings did not consist of a single person in a pulpit talking for an hour with no questions or other response! Nor were those single persons put on a pedestal.

I suppose the objective of this book is to question traditionalism and to seek a better, more dynamic way, to live as believers, without imbibing or practicing those obnoxious activities known in so many churches. Some traditions are good and useful, but most are corrupt.

The arguments will come from scripture; I have no interest whatever in promoting my own ideas. Do we want Christ to rule, or men? Forget about 'doing church' – instead just live as Christ requires us to live.

Note: In this book reference is made to traumatic situations and changes which put young men at a disadvantage. Elders (pastors) should be older men, not young people. Many modern 'pastors' do not comply with this biblical model, and a large number enter Bible colleges almost from school, so have no life experience. It is true that when God gives us tasks to do He will provide the knowledge and skills.

But, God does not go against His own definition of who is a pastor/elder/presbyter/bishop.

The Old Testament speaks of not just older men, but 'ancient' men! The New Testament model does not differ. For example, Matthew uses ***presbyteros***, meaning older in age, advanced in life, a senior. Luke uses ***prebyterion***, to describe men who were older. The same meanings apply throughout both Testaments, often with the idea of 'grey-haired'. Clearly, men who are young should not be pastors. Yet, pastorates are filled with them. I do not question their zeal or desires, but they simply don't fit what scripture says. (See later section on pastors). And this is only one objection to modern traditionalism.

A very simple definition of this bad tradition is 'Anything said or done that does not arise naturally from scripture, or that is added to or removed from what scripture says'.

Perhaps, if you have been in a traditionalist church for years (as I was), you might have a knee-jerk reaction and put this book aside. It is too much to take in! But, I assure you that everything said is true, and what I refer to has been experienced by myself and many others. Sometimes God will move a person out of his comfort zone dramatically, and sometimes He will do so slowly, until the final light switches on, and you say "Enough is enough. I must stop this. Then, you find a local church that actually acts in godly fashion and teaches God's word without denominational or traditionalist fashion.

As you read though the book, muse upon what happens in your own local church. See if what I say makes sense scripturally. Then try to apply it to your own situation. The Lord will one day demand to know why so many remain silent whilst traditionalism replaces genuine worship. The Toronto Blessing did this with bells on! Do not follow bad traditions – live dynamically and authentically!

Chapter 1

Undoing the False Church

In this section I look at the way God took us along a path that was hitherto alien to us, because, like so many others, we were fed on traditionalist soup, which lacked in nutrition. Therefore, there is a mixture in this book of personal catharsis, amazing scriptural revelation – not new, because it is all there in black and white, but was 'invisible' to a traditional eye. Along the way, I/we underwent great changes, some of them remarkable and surprising, and some traumatic – swimming against the tide can be exhausting.

My life has been filled by wondrous times, but also a steady bombardment of traumas, horrible scenarios, horrific happenings, and so on, including near-death illnesses and physical attacks on my person. It is a fact that many Western Christians live life in tranquility and so they know nothing of hardship, ongoing fears and nasty surprises. They have nothing authentic to follow.

Theirs is a false tranquility; rather, it is a hiding-away from spiritual reality. Many 'great' names of the past have commented that Christian lives that suffer nothing and risk nothing are hardly worth living, because they do nothing.

However, do not make the mistake of thinking that my amazingly complex life situations have formed my pastorate. No, I just pastor according to scripture, so all the traumatic experiences are 'add-ons'. Christians who attempt to follow God as He demands tend to have a similar background, because Satan hates believers who are genuine and faithful! He will attack them time and again.

As I have already noted, I was brought up in a church atmosphere. From birth I was taken to services morning and/or evening, and sometimes on weekdays; at times to go with my mother and aunt who sang duets in evening services. So, by the time I was in my teens I was familiar with the chat, activities and atmosphere of 'church', even though I had no idea what it all meant. I just did what everyone else was doing. No right, no wrong, just do the activity and go home! (Which is what most Christians do today).

It was all normal to me and I 'went with the flow'. In my mid-teens I attended the adult Sunday School class, where in 1965 I was literally caught by God's hand in a remarkable way, when I was cynical and loved to argue. That day when I left the meeting about 4pm, a fellow teenager asked if I was going to hand myself over to God. I told him I didn't feel ready. He replied that if I left it to my feelings I would NEVER be ready. He was right. Then, as I walked back home in summer sunshine I was commanded by God to go to my bedroom to pray. It was a voice 'in my head' that took priority. I did so and was saved. That evening I asked to be baptized. After that summer surprise, everything changed. Before my salvation I accepted everything said and done by fellow members, elders and pastors. AFTER my salvation I quickly began to question what was said and done! I had no idea of theology or even of real Bible study, but my mind was captured by God.

I was unable to just accept what I had accepted for the previous 18 years. But, I found no answers, and did not even know how to ask the questions. I just knew something wasn't right. Readers might query this, but I would say that I was 'onboard' with everything said to me. Why should I suddenly begin to question my brand-new faith and what was going on around me? It didn't come from within... otherwise, I would have been a dissident for my previous churchgoing years.

Also, though I had serious questions to ask, I didn't really know WHAT to ask. And when I DID ask, I was 'shut down', politely but firmly! To put it bluntly, I underwent the slow process of just listening and keeping my mouth shut, whether the issue was serious or not; a perfect scenario for learning my skills as a traditionist! Again, I went along with the others so as to maintain some sort of 'fellowship'. (Obviously, there is no 'fellowship' where one is compelled to keep silent and not to rock the boat. Sadly, though, this is what happens in most churches, where a band-aid of silence covers many queries and doubts. It is all pretense, if not spiritual fraud. Think about it).

This spiritual and intellectual awkwardness 'rumbled on' in the background for the next 20 years, as my mind and heart were at variance with what I heard and saw. That was when I began to preach and teach Bible classes at home (1966). I was thirsty for knowledge and had a constant stream of theological queries in my head, though I did not know they were 'theological'.

For the first ten years I thought it was 'just me', but the questions kept coming. So, they fomented in my mind and heart for yet another ten years. Also, for those twenty years, I obeyed the reformed way of life and methods used to teach. It took all that time to realise I was being an automaton, foolishly following what was tradition and not scripture. And so my mind and heart were being eroded by false beliefs, even though they had the tag of 'Christian' attached.

Like so many others, I thought the pastor was the 'boss' in charge of us all. For this reason I attempted to copy the pastor and elders (before I saw that elders and pastors were the same thing) so that I complied with the traditionalist approach to 'doing church' – my outward demeanor was the same as everyone else's, but my spirit was deeply troubled, increasingly so, as it did inward battle with my human soul. I was quite bad at copying my peers, who, no doubt, secretly agreed amongst themselves!

I attempted to put it right, but each time I tried to do so I was shut down, as those faithful to tradition refused to listen. Today, having been a pastor for about 40 years, I continue to shed the traditionalist view of what and who a pastor is, because the job of change is not yet complete, and from what I can see, never will. It is a vital task.

Oh how my perception changed as the Holy Spirit guided me along a different path... in my head I followed whatever was the reformed path, but in my heart and spirit I was becoming more and more confused by trying to follow both the path given to me by the Spirit And the one forged by tradition! When a man says he is 'Reformed' it is a statement of the past, propping-up a near-dead spirit. But, if he keeps on reforming, he is <u>continuing</u> what the reformers began, and has a lively and eager spirit.

The Spirit led me truly, but I didn't know how to resolve the situation. And because everyone else followed traditionalism like sheep, so did I. But, the days of doing so became riddled with questions and no answers. The day I completely left the traditional path/system was traumatic but exciting and it led to me 'undoing' church (as perceived by men) rather than 'doing' it (as taught by God's word)! I first had to ditch traditionalism before I could move on.

I can illustrate this feeling by looking at old rural roads in Malta. My wife and I used to laugh when we took a small hire car across the island. As we drove we got used to the bumpiness as the car went over pot holes we studiously tried to avoid; an impossible task! I described them as a lace covering – holes joined together by very thin and sparse mud and dirt!

This image is like the widespread influence of traditionalism. It is spread so thin that the surface teachings are hardly joined by God's word. In places the spiritual 'pot holes' became too big to travel over so teachings can be isolated and seemingly unconnected to truth.

You might ask how I knew this was of the Holy Spirit and not just deviance in my mind. I can only say that as the end of the twenty years arrived I was fast becoming disillusioned and very concerned. It was as if I was being forced to face my future, while being thrust into a funnel! Not by what others did and said but by what happened within myself. To be frank, I could have continued as before just as others do until they die, but my spirit was troubled by useless traditions. It HAD to come to an end, but I didn't know how or when.

I believe that was when God brought me to a 'crunch-point'... I was unable to detect what was wrong, so couldn't do anything about it. A malady can't be treated unless it is first diagnosed! Since being saved, over the decades, I have discovered that God really does move in mysterious ways! Over time I have prayed for God to give answers to a variety of questions and situations, and, every time, the answers came in the most surprising of ways! And this is how I lost any preference for traditionalism. As I have sometimes said to others – why should I keep hold of what is less when I have been given something that is much more?

Time to Change

I have told of this matter before, but will repeat it now, because it explains part of my attitude at that time.

As I was preaching regularly, in Wales and England, I was invited to a kind of preachers' forum in our church, by my then pastor. As I sat in that first (and last – I was obviously not of traditional preacher material!) meeting of fellow preachers, I felt uncomfortable, but listened; I was certainly not encouraged. Soon after that I was asked to speak at the mid-week Bible study as a test of my calibre. I chose my text, wrote my study, and spoke at the meeting amidst a cool but respectful silence. That's when it seemed to start falling apart...

I had an admiration for the other preachers and tried my very best to copy them. And that was my downfall! The men I tried to copy were good believers, BUT, I was NOT them! Instead of allowing God to tell me what He wanted <u>me</u> to say and do, I was a mere copyist, trying to be like someone else. For that reason I failed miserably as a 'fellow preacher', though I used the same 'techniques'.

After some time I became uncomfortable in my spiritual skin, and told a few other young men. That was a mistake, because I then became a rebel in their eyes. They said I had to obey the pastor and elders and could not do what came into my mind, even though I honestly told them I had to do what GOD told me to do, and I was convinced He told me to begin a new ministry. My 'acceptance' soon started to disappear! In their minds I was declining and showing signs of 'backsliding'. But, I could not stop my mind or spirit from disobeying 'tradition'.

Toilet, or Sleep?
Then, as I wriggled like a worm on a hook, God showed me a far better way by using His key to my understanding. On its own it might sound like a ridiculous thing, but, to me, it was the biggest revelation to that time (I have spoken of this before)! The key unlocked a door I was unable to shut again. Indeed, I never even knew there WAS a door!

There comes a point in life where a particular word or action completely surprises a man, so that he can never again return to what was former. What was that key? It was simple in the extreme, but to me it was the start of my spiritual freedom in Christ. Some might laugh at it, but everything clicked into place...

It came down to one single Bible verse. My class at home was going with me through the book of 1 Samuel. As usual this was built around detailed study of commentaries and scripture, examined on my days off from work. This happened to be every night as well as on days off. (The Lord's work is all-consuming and has no time limits).

One evening we reached the part where king Saul entered the Adullam cave (1 Samuel 24) where, unknown to him, David and his 400 warriors were hiding from Saul's soldiers. This came after months of being chased through the deserts. The verse that rocked my world and began my new life, was 24:3.

> *"And he came to the sheepcotes by the way,*
> *where was a cave; and Saul went in to cover*
> *his feet: and David and his men remained in*
> *the sides of the cave."*

Readers will probably read that text and ask "So? Why is this verse significant?" Well, there are times when God speaks directly to a believer in a personal way. Yes, we all have the same biblical texts before us, but God will use a familiar text like a spiritual lightning bolt! It only means something to that one person, while others are bemused.

To others it might seem nothing, but for twenty years I had delivered sermons and Bible studies as I thought fit. I attempted to copy my peers. I read the usual commentaries and even used the 'Geneva pulpit' style of preaching. And I have even preached in churches where a line of elders sat behind me, scrutinising everything I said. Now, as I sat transfixed, that single verse alerted me to a far greater revelation of God and how He worked in my life. What made it so significant and life-changing?

It was this... the brief phrase "covered his feet" showed me how to interpret the situation between Saul and David. Yes, others will shake their heads and say "Yes, I KNOW about that interpretation". But, at that time I DIDN'T know! And being shown the meaning was literally a life-changing moment.

To my amazement, I discovered that the phrase has one of two meanings in Hebrew; that Saul had entered the cave to pass water/empty his bowels, OR, to go to sleep. This was the key to interpretation of that text... using what I now refer to as 'biblical logic' I saw that it could not possibly mean he had entered to relieve himself, so it had to mean he entered to sleep, out of the blazing sun.

How do I know this? Because David and 400 men were hiding in that cave. If one of them even breathed heavily the sound would have echoed loudly around the cave. Also, there is no way that David could otherwise have crept up on Saul to cut off the end of his clothing! So, Saul entered to sleep. Nowadays such a simple interpretation is accepted easily enough, but, at that time, it came to me as an amazing revelation.

After that I began to study Hebraisms and forms of Hebrew (I am only now teaching myself how to read Hebrew). And, along with my brother, I took a course in Koine Greek. After that time, revelation upon revelation poured like a torrent from scripture itself. In other words, I discovered that my relationship with God was dynamic and His word was filled with ongoing truths. And over time this led to my now familiar approach:

1. Usually, the meaning in the original language gives the interpretation.
2. Each interpretation depends mainly (but not always) on context. Almost every word in scripture has several or more possible meanings.
3. Where I honestly cannot see an interpretation, I either leave it for the moment, or I look at what trusted commentators might have said (this is now very rare). Even then, I might disagree because their interpretation does not convince me.
4. Always, the final interpretation depends on the Holy Spirit.

With the above as a guide, over the years I slowly left my commentaries aside and relied on God to guide my thoughts. For too long I relied instead on other men, my peers, and commentaries. As I continued I could see that even the best commentators sometimes got it wrong, or gave answers to which I could not concur. My knowledge and understanding grew, thanks be to God.

So, that single phrase in a single verse turned my life around so sharply it left my head spinning! Instead of trying to teach and preach by copying 'peer reviewed' traditionalistic sources, I began to preach and teach with an entirely new ethos – one given by God Himself in His own word. I was astounded that I was locked-into traditionalism in the first place, and quickly started to dismantle my whole way of thinking. Today, what I think and write complies with what I came to know, and the way I presented it.

The Beginning of BTM

Then, in 1985, my new ministry began, with an explosive expose of what came to be known as AIDS. This was when I found out, in a shocking way, that telling the truth brings enemies more than it brings friends! Just two friends again stood by me – Peter Trumper and Arthur Harris. To his credit, Arthur, a longstanding Pentecostal minister, changed his life after reading my work on charismaticism: he began by casting away so-called 'tongues' as an 'angelic language'. I know this because, to his credit, he humbly told me.

Most 'ministers', however, disowned me, our new small church, and the ministry. Indeed, it was so bad in my home town, that a number of Pentecostalists and 'reformed' accepted my studies (in the CRI Pack) but begged me not to send them by post, just in case their families found out! In some cases I had to deliver them covertly at night to the actual addresses! Such was the fear of traditionalism and fellow peers! (There is much more to this period).

Now, after over 35 years of the BTM ministry and our earlier church founding, the ministry is strong as ever, is read more by readers outside our city than within the city (indeed, worldwide), such was the disaffection by others and, at times, sheer hatred. No-one likes to know their beliefs are untrue or skewed badly, and are mistaken or even heretical. Thus, they often hit-out in anger. This is why, today, almost no Christians in our city speak to me; if we meet they politely move away from me. And all of them know nothing of my ministry or beliefs! My infamy goes before me! Based on nothing but grumbling and rumour.

For such folks what I was doing was unforgivable. I was tearing apart the very basis for their faith (or so they thought; I was actually dismantling the traditionalism that wrongly influenced their faith). As a Christian I once knew said, if I revealed the truth there would be nothing left! And he was almost correct. Nevertheless, BTM and our church moved together, one critical of the other, because BTM was an extension of the church. Whatever I say or write is under the influence of our church.

I slowly began to question everything I once knew, in great detail. A number of 'huge' topics were studied, not from the stance of my peers or tradition, but from scripture itself. These included prayer meetings, pastors, services, the two ordained commands of communion and baptism, how meetings should be, and so on.

Alongside these came sudden demands from the Spirit to tackle such things as charismaticism, homosexuality, false environmentalism, Islam, and, in 2020-1, the fake pandemic of Covid-19. All vital, with a definite beginning and end (except for the Covid scandal, which has not finished its course at time of writing). All these are discussed in our church meetings as well as published, and some of the topics are also published as books. And, as expected, these are studied and accepted and retaught to others, by pastors around the world... but, not in my home city!

Only once did I receive a criticism that caused me to remove an article, which praised something said by a teacher from the USA. At the time I did not know of certain heresies he taught. The article was promptly taken down with an apology. As for my articles/books on biblical topics, I have not yet received true criticism.

Yes, some will complain because I step on their denominational toes. But, there have been no actual criticisms of my Bible interpretations, simply because I follow the strict 'method' already discussed... where interpretation is found in the meanings of words given in Hebrew and Greek (or sometimes in Aramaic, especially the book of Daniel). That is, the

Bible itself gives the interpretation. A few will loathe the interpretation, not because there are any biblical errors, but because they do not like my conclusions or my general set of beliefs! It is a sad fact that most preachers teach 'spiritualised' texts – flowery texts that serve to cover-up poor exegesis that has very little meaning, if any at all.

As you might expect, these background facts determine the activity and ethos of our church, all of whom are saved men and women. We also have a Sunday School (see later comments on the concept of Sunday Schools). Our church meetings are unique and unknown to almost all other believers, who tend to remain in the clutches of traditionalism. This is because, after leaving the 'system', we agreed with God's command, to gather-together as He taught and not as we wish. All of this comes directly from God's word not our own minds! Anything we don't know is kept aside until we know better.

In other words, we try to comply with what God teaches and not with what is found throughout 'Christendom'. Thus, we accept that God's word must dictate what we say and do, and do not follow useless traditions.

There are a few good traditions, but most modern churches are built upon mistaken traditions (traditionalism and not scripture; to be a 'good' tradition is to allow repeated practices to arise naturally from scripture), and it is the former which we reject. Now and then, for specific reasons and rarely, we might attend a local church that is in the 'system' (e.g. a memorial service), but now it all seems alien to scripture and we feel uncomfortable.

This is what allegiance to God actually means. It is certainly not the road of comfort, but is a road of hardship at times, as we want to follow God and not men, who look upon us with suspicion!

Next, we will look at how we, as a local church, conduct ourselves. Most readers will not understand it, nor will they approve, because it doesn't meet with their traditionalist expectations. And those who attend as visitors rarely return! It is disconcerting to them to be too close to others, and to hear godly teaching, as an 'unknown' variation of all they have been taught by traditionalism. Later, I will present several evidences of this.

In the 'run up' to leaving the system, we changed churches three times, then the fourth change was to leave altogether. The details of WHY we changed and why we left are interesting and were done to adhere to scripture. It seems God sped us swiftly through this process! (If you need those details I can provide them, but will not state who or where those churches are. Nor would I mention names of errant pastors. There is no need to breach confidentiality). Suffice to say that the need for the changes was important, and were not done on a whim or by personal emotions.

If you discovered, say, that a medicine you were taking was actually making your illness worse... would you stop taking it, or continue because others implored you to do so? (Like the fake 'vaccines' pretending to protect against a false Covid virus).

If you took your shoes off and deliberately walked on broken glass so your feet were shredded... would you stop doing it and let your feet heal? Yet, so many continue to practice false doctrine and traditionalism, to their spiritual harm.

If you sat under a ministry for years and the preacher/pastor began to teach heresy... would you (a) recognize it was heresy and (b) would you complain and advise the speaker (c) and leave that church if he continued with heresy? Sadly, most do not. Are you able to distinguish fact from fiction, truth from lies, true doctrine from heresy?

It is a very sad fact that most Christians are in traditionalist churches and do not complain or query when a preacher teaches untruths, or heresy. This is because they feel comfortable socially. Those of us who left this system also felt comfortable, but God has a way to make us very much uncomfortable. He will keep on doing this until we examine our hearts and minds, and carefully investigate all our beliefs and behaviour.

Once we KNOW something is wrong we are duty-bound to cast it aside, or attend a different church.

Would YOU? We did not leave the last 'system' church we attended because the young pompous 'pastor' told lies about us to a farmer. We also left 'his' church (many pastors think the local churches are 'theirs') because he was on the edge of teaching heresy. We either left or we would have faced an explosive situation, where we went head-on with someone filled with pride.

Make no mistake – most churches for several centuries have become staid and solidified, relying only on past achievements. Some are churches that began at the height of remarkable revivals. But, a local church is only as valid and alive as its present members. It cannot exist on the memory of sound believers of the past. To put it bluntly, if no member and pastors are saved and act accordingly, it is NOT a local church, but only a hazy memory of one. It is of no value.

Chapter 2

How <u>We</u> 'Do' Church

I don't usually use the term 'doing church', but, like slang, it is standard parlance, and so it is the only reason I use it. I would prefer to call it 'being obedient to God'. To say 'doing church' is to objectify and externalize what it means to be one of the true ekklesia, the elect. What I now relate is how WE began our church under God, and continue to do so. It can be a suitable example to follow, or not. You and your fellows must decide for yourselves, after prayer and meditation. If you want extra details of any part referred to in this book, just ask... this book is only a summary.

When my family left the 'system' it was not because we wanted to start a movement or even a local church. Nor was it caused by feeling angry, or upset, or somehow 'superior'. Far from it! The final change came about because the local church 'leaders' were so distanced from God's word, or from decent brotherly behaviour, we had no real choice but to follow the Holy spirit's demands and were compelled to leave. The attitudes, teachings and personal dislike for us shown by the other local churches, made it impossible to stay in any of them, and it is very likely God used our circumstances and experiences to move us out of our comfort zones. We were disliked because we no longer went along with traditionalism. But, more than that, we knew God was calling us to live truly in the freedom of Christ.

> *"There is therefore now no condemnation to them which are in Christ Jesus, who walk not after the flesh, but after the Spirit."* (Romans 8:1)

Personally, each of us had "had enough" of pretense. How God speaks to others is His concern, and we have no ulterior or proud reasons to leave traditionalism behind. We owed it to the Lord. It took God-given courage to leave the 'system', because it was a scary time!

The "Spirit of life in Christ Jesus hath made me free from the law of sin and death" (Romans 8:2)… so why persist in walking the wrong path?

Surely we were deluding ourselves? Maybe some think this way, but it isn't what happened: "I say the truth in Christ, I lie not, my conscience also bearing me witness in the Holy Ghost." (Romans 9:1).

We no longer relied on the traditionalist fairy-tale, but in the hard-nosed facts of God's word. We wanted our faith to flow from truth in our hearts to truth in the future: "If in this life only we have hope in Christ, we are of all men most miserable." (1 Corinthians 15:19). Sadly, many who claim salvation are fine with the little they have, given by a false tradition, but such a life is alien to what is to come – going to live in the Heavenly abode of El Shaddai. And this assurance does not come through traditionalism!

To put it bluntly, those pastors who 'had rule' over us were despicably foul toward us and did not tolerate any form of questioning or dissidence… a dissidence brought about by their own mishandling of scripture and their behaviour… traditionalism-plus! The unfortunate fact about this is that the churches we left were 'normal' and constitute the average traditionalist church system, so they are just a small number of the total, who all act the same way. They all obey 'group-speak'!

The Final Circumstance
What prompted us to finally leave the entire system came about thus: We were in a particular church that had a very young pastor, who evidently believed he was incredibly biblical, yet he thought nothing of us as people. He stated that we all owed him reverence because of his 'reverend' status, regardless of his personal failings or sins. He also loved to tell his congregation that he knew something they didn't, so implying his theological superiority!

And I still remember his terrible decision to speak against one deacon who refused to stand for singing, in protest at the pastor's dictatorial attitudes, with everyone in the congregation witnessing his tirade. If he had anything against the man (who I knew to have been a quiet and gentle person), he should have spoken with him privately. Enough is enough!

Even before we began to attend 'his' church (the very one I was saved in many years before) the previous pastor of the church we just left told him how awful we were. (I will refrain from giving details in this book, but the reasons for leaving 'his' church were biblically sound). This pastor-to-pastor divulging of personal details with no opportunity to give the 'other side' of the story is prevalent amongst churches… it gives a decided advantage to pastors and churches, rather like a spiritual mafia. In these fraternals much backstabbing goes on, with a great deal of slander, but always said "in love".

The time to leave the final church came after the pastor went to preach in a West Wales rural church. On the day he preached he went back to a deacon's farmhouse for a meal. What he did NOT know was that we knew the farmer and his wife, and were friends with them.

The pastor had a meal and began to tell the farmer of us as a family, painting us in the most vivid terms as backsliders and heretics. What he did NOT know was that the farmer switched on a tape machine when he began to derogate us. A few days later, we heard what the pastor had said about us, and it wasn't good! It was also a pack of lies. And so we decided to leave. Or, more accurately, God gave us reason to get out..

There was no way we could remain after such a wicked act of tittle-tattle, where a pastor and deacons tolerated us because they had no idea how to get rid of us… so they lied instead and smiled to our faces. Everyone thought we were just being backslidden and heretical, but the damage had been done so there was no benefit in pleading our case, or even telling the 'pastor' we knew all about his conversation.

Leaving the System

What we did next was both funny and weird! As I have already stated, everybody had decided to elect me pastor and simply presented me with the *fete accompli*. I must admit I did not particularly want to be a pastor, but it was their wish and it was not a time to argue about it. Yet, I received many verifications from the Lord in the next few weeks.

Everyone was perturbed by the sudden upheaval, because we had left a system we had been brought up in – some of us for our entire lives. The hierarchy was still fresh in our minds, as was the typical traditional 'churchy stuff' we were so used to. But, the overbearing arrogance of the final former pastors, and the hypocritical 'friendliness' of the last one, gave us an odd courage.

The last four churches we attended (the one before the last one, had INVITED us to go to his church, even after hearing why we had to leave) were so unwelcoming and totalitarian, teaching so many errors, rapidly ate away at any obedience we once thought we owed them. And so there we were, up to less than thirty individuals including children, unable to enter another local church because our images and characters were so maligned.

It took a while to realize that we were not <u>forced</u> out by the churches, but <u>led</u> out by God… we were so obedient to the system that He had to give us a shock to move! As I have already intimated, two good friends in pastorates encouraged us to move away from the system: 'Rev' Peter Trumper and 'Rev' Arthur Harris. They were always in the background giving encouragement, and though both are now with the Lord, I thank them for their love.

Addendum

When I was writing this section, I attended a memorial service in a 'system' church we had been forced to leave about forty years ago. Sadly, it reminded me of why I left in the first place. Nothing in the system changes.

The Next Three Years

From the start people asked how we could possibly "do church" when we were "no longer in a church". The very phrases were themselves invalid, for 'doing church' implies an organization external to the spirit. Each Christian is a perpetual, automatic member of the universal Church, even if they don't attend a local church meeting. As a gathering, then, we <u>were</u> the Church when we met. We were <u>always</u> a genuine *ekklesia,* and still are. But, it took a while to realise this! We were like drug addicts who were 'going cold turkey' and our new situation would take a few years to sink in. Even today, almost 40 years later, I am still trying to 'get it right'… my apprenticeship is not yet over so I must keep learning!

In the first week of leaving we were all wondering what on earth we were now going to do. It was a peculiar feeling! Some were anxious, as if oxygen had been cut off. So, we talked about it at great length. We all agreed that our hearts were with Christ but our minds were still with the system devised by men. This helped, but the scorn and anger directed at us for daring to leave continued for a long time, though we had done nothing wrong. (Which is why I can sympathise with Job).

We Left the System NOT the Church!
It took about three years to get over this odd feeling of 'leaving the Church'… but we soon realized that NOBODY can 'leave the Church' because 'once saved always saved'. We came to see that we did not 'leave the church' – we left a <u>system</u>, a man-made organization and activities. It was just a 'bad habit' and, like any addict, we had to wean ourselves from taking the useless mllk.

It is a fact that we rarely had meat, enabling us to grow, and we only ate what singular pastors gave to us from the store-cupboard. And like Oliver Twist we were always hungry. With this is mind, we then began to look at every single aspect of 'church', with in-depth examination. No longer could we simply accept what one man said (including myself) as true, when what was said contradicted God's word.

At times we were genuinely shocked by what we had once imbibed and continued to do, but we did not do anything in those years unless we had completed a thorough investigation. We did this by simply reading God's word and discovering meanings and interpretations as the word dictated. No doubt many Christians and pastors THINK this is what they do… but our times in a number of local churches proved otherwise. This became glaringly obvious when it came to studying prayer meetings.

As with every other doctrinal issues, we did nothing until we examined every aspect. At the end of this book I show the BTM Publications' List, containing everything published up to the end of December, 2021. This contains just about everything we discussed in the years following leaving. We studied each book of the New Testament and are still going through all of the Old. It is published in the book to show our conclusions and sources, complete with biblical texts.

It took me quite some time to write up my findings to present to the members (only saved people can be members), and what we discovered by studying God's word alone, was that prayer meetings as we know them today are invalid, if not harmful to God's people, and a dishonour to the Lord. The substance of this finding is given in a later chapter. Of course, our conclusions are hotly disputed by traditionalists, but we had to adhere to what we believe God has shown us.

We Examined Everything

Alongside this were studies of many other traditionalistic 'beliefs' that were more habits and not true beliefs... the pastor, elders and deacons; communion; membership; buildings, and so on. Everything was scrutinized, even though some aspects were very hard to deal with. A little later, I took one aspect further by preparing for my doctorate. Over the years I had studied personally, taken many Bible courses, and took relevant exams in them.

I began PhD studies with Trinity – many pastors in the UK were with them; after two years I was asked to be the UK Alumni Director. For two years I completed all assignments, earning A+ for each. I had to stop with Trinity at a time when I was unable to pay for my studies: I had another reason after learning of certain beliefs of the president. So, later, I signed-up with another university and earned my PhD with a dissertation on Disfellowship.

This came about after completing several degrees in education and psychology, one at Master's level. They were all pertinent to our general examination of all things 'church'*. In 1981 I read a short tract on pastors, based on scriptural texts, by Jon Zens. It revolutionized my thoughts on the subject and caused me to finally cast aside the traditionist view and teaching, particularly as I wanted to be a pastor according to scripture and not according to the views and traditions of other men.

(*A modified CV is available, giving the 'bare bones' of my education and qualifications, etc. However, do not think that qualifications prove a man's suitability for the pastorate. Or, that a Bible college training fits a man to be a pastor).

The end of our searching period saw a very different group of Christians from those who left the system! Our conclusions, founded only on scripture, made us immensely strong and confident in God's word and our own leaving of the 'system' (which was instigated by God in the first place). In this way we became a genuine local church.

We dabbled with a name, but dropped it; we were and still are a local manifestation of the church in our city. Call us a 'house church' if you wish, but it is a valid local church that meets in a house and has lasted for 35 years so far! Simple.

We did not apologise to other Christians for leaving the system, or for the way we have Sunday meetings, which is VERY different from meetings in the system! We have never advertised our presence, believing that numbers mean nothing, and people would join us if God led them.

Unfortunately, along the way some attached themselves to us with enthusiasm but left within weeks, or even one or two years. As the saying goes, they could not 'hack it', especially if they were expecting the same concrete meetings as they had once known, or, they refused to align their beliefs with scripture. Later, we interviewed folks who thought they wanted to join us. It's a matter of honesty, and people come and go. After all, the local church is a collection of saved people, whether they come for one meeting or stay for many.

No Sermons
Many are unsure of the non-format of our meetings (because there is none), the study of whole books in depth, and the personal relationships created just by sitting closer together! Nor can they get used to frequent interruptions during the study period, with comments, queries and even objections. Meetings are in my home; adults meet together in one room and children in another. At times we are all crammed in together... no problem! None of this would be tolerated in a 'system' church.

Most paid pastors try not to 'rock the boat', because they might otherwise lose members, and this would lead to fewer cash gifts! Some have openly admitted to me that they deliberately do not touch certain subjects because they would lead to contention. In our view this is unholy nonsense – we tackle difficult topics head-on, hopefully with love and care. We never avoid them. It is all or nothing, because that is what God's word demands. And, as I am not paid, I do not avoid sensitive issues anyway. For this reason some have gone from us, but, that is not of importance so long as those who stay obey God and not me or any other foundation. It is important to be true to God, regardless of discomfort we might have.

We do not have sermons, where one man speaks for an hour whilst everyone else sits still, trying to open sweet wrappers soundlessly, or even closing their eyes (I am not surprised). If someone wants to eat a sweet – let them do so! If they close their eyes… so what? No young man has fallen from an upstairs window, so we are okay for now! Therefore, we have no 'pack drill' and we are all equal with no silencing. We sometimes laugh when something is funny, but at all times we are cognizant of the fact that we are meeting in God's Name.

Their Choice
It was decided from the very start that the members wanted in-depth Bible studies, going through books of the Bible. And that is what I do. Every Sunday other matters are brought up; if dealing with these takes a long time, then the Bible study is rescheduled for 'if and when'. This is because what I do in the meeting is according to the group and God, not me; I am not more important than the

others, nor is what I teach necessarily of top importance on the day.

As I deliver the study, members are encouraged to ask questions, make comments, and even disagree. In this way there is true communal spirit and an open invite to speak... every study time is more of a flowing discussion. (Try interrupting a speaker in full swing in a 'system' church!). If we do not complete the study that week, it does not matter, because it can be resumed later.

As for prayer... we do not have those weekly planned 'prayer meetings', which shocks some. Nor do we have prayer sessions before, during, or after the meeting. Like other things, prayer is treated as we see it in scripture.

On rare occasions, when required, we might corporately pray earnestly for a particular urgent matter. In other words, we pray as we see it is dealt with in scripture. And we also pray individually at any time. This is hard for many visitors to understand, but after deep study of the subject, we conclude we are acting according to God's word. A key to it all is the command by Christ to pray alone in our room. (For more, see my book, 'Prayer Meetings')

Other Aspects
We began our new church by studying 'church' meetings. That is, a gathering of saved souls, the true *ekklesia* (the word does not only apply to

churches – it can mean ANY gathering, even of unbelievers; hence the qualifying word, 'true', etc). The unsaved may attend but they are not members and we do not spend whole meetings talking only to the unsaved. This is because church meetings are just for the church – saved individuals. In many ways, then, any unsaved people in our midst are observers. It is up to God to move their hearts or not.

Today, after about 40 years, we are still examining every aspect of scripture and, even now, we come across fresh revelations in the word itself. (No, we are NOT charismatic!). To put it basically, we believe everything in scripture and teach it as it is presented to us by God.   Literal is literal, poetic is poetic, figurative is figurative. Historical is historical.

Thus, for example, though we consider ourselves to be more-or-less 'reformed', we do not accept that the gifts and wonders are now totally gone. This is because scripture provides no proof that the Lord has finished with them. Rather, the opposite is true. (Here I am not referring to the fakery of charismaticism). Also, biblical logic tells us that the very words of the New Testament show that certain gifts remain – salvation itself, repentance, faith, etc., because they are very obviously still with us.

On the other hand, certain things must be spoken against, such as the charismatic teachings on 'angelic tongues' and the idea of a semi-secretive 'second dose of the Spirit'.

Once the Lord had established us as a genuine church, God moved me along another line of action – the formation of Bible Theology Ministries. It started by noticing discrepancies in research on what later became known as AIDS (1980s). At the time I was a lecturer in a university college, teaching health topics to professionals. The research took me about three years and was approved by the departmental head (who retracted her support when the research was hated by homosexuals!).

I was registered with the DHSS to receive daily reports and contacted a number of worldwide agencies to gather information, including one in Russian. I discovered that what government was saying was a lie and deception! (Much as government is now doing with the false 'pandemic' of Covid-19 and its claimed 'remedy', false vaccines). I chased the links and found a glaringly wicked decision to uphold homosexuals, who were the original cause of AIDS, and yet were being protected from public scrutiny and blame.

Then, as today, anyone who questioned the official statements was sacked, or otherwise silenced, much of it by scorn and derision from homosexuals. There were no scientific objections to my findings! Of course, with so many homosexuals in parliament, and the inordinate influence of homosexual groups, MPs wanted to hush the real facts. One minister said that if people only knew the truth there would be a big backlash. He was right, but he was not allowed to speak out again. For more on this tragic deception see other materials I wrote. The things I discovered were so blatant and deceptive I felt I had to let others know the truth, particularly Christians. This we did by publishing what we called the 'CRI Pack'.

But, people do not want truth. Within days I was sacked from my lecturing job, which would have included becoming Director of Health Research in a few months, and UK-wide attacks by homosexuals and others, including a well-known Christian publication that openly scorned and hated me while they upheld an homosexual 'pastor' for 'coming out'. Death threats soon followed and I lost my job and academic career.

I made a number of predictions (NOT prophecies) based entirely on known facts and the obvious path the disease had to take. Though scorned, each prediction came true within two years. But, GPs and health staff were all tutored in the 'facts according to homosexuality'. None of them were allowed to research for themselves and everyone was talking from the same source. In this way, dissident views were crushed quickly and hatred for those of us who spoke out became loud and fast-moving. The same strategy is being used as I write, concerning Covid19.

Even so, I was compelled by God to keep going. The hate and violence that came my way was beyond understanding, and it still comes to my doorstep. This is when other Christians said it was my own fault that I was being harassed and attacked. I should have just kept quiet! The result of all this is now with us in hellish ways and by not opposing homosexual growth, we now suffer the natural result – homosexual laws, hatred for Christians, and increasing demand to allow all kinds of sexual deviance, including in schools. The freshest new kid on the block is transgenderism.

As you might imagine this 'hot-house' environment became a part of my spiritual character-building, and affected everything I did, and still do, in our church. All of it, to my mind, is given by God for a purpose. Any pastor might be called to such front-line opposition, and this will always affect the pastoral role and the local church.

That was the start of BTM ministry. It was quickly joined by other topics I was led to research and write about. Peter Trumper thought the first edition of the Pack was explosive and full of detail, but thought I "could not keep it up". He meant that I could not keep finding such amazingly spectacular material to write about.

Though his advice on this would have been right in any secular activity, I did not set out to begin the BTM ministry... God sent it to me in such a way I could not refuse! And what I write about is always led by God, not my own choices. Sometimes God's choice is a complete surprise to me, and sometimes I am reluctant to follow it up. But, we all know what happened to Jonah!

The first edition brought fear and anxiety for a while (including loss of job and death threats). I certainly was not looking to lose my job and begin a new ministry (BTM). Rather, the new ministry (now 36 years old) is an outgrowth of our church meetings. Thus, members receive each new article and study and scrutinize contents. This is because I am subject to every other member of our local church, as well as to the Church universal.

Topics Sent by God
The BTM is still publishing hard-nosed material, but I have never looked for something to write about – everything I write is demanded of me by God! I cannot refuse. In this way the initial nuclear blast of dealing with homosexual AIDS became an ongoing issue, until something else took prime place – and along came charismatic heresy (the Toronto Blessing); the fake environmental issue (supposed global warming); a number of years warning about Islam and its effects on the world, and more.

The latest issue pressed upon me is Covid-19. It has caused immense fear amongst Christians and others, so, as I did with AIDS, I researched the issue and read many worldwide reports, before telling Christians what was really going on (the subjecting of all people to socialism and One World government), using fear of a fake pandemic to force even Christians to have a 'vaccine' that is just as fake as the pandemic. Before explaining it to fellow believers I took a Covid course with London university, so as to know my subject.

There is far more to the present issue, but this book is not about the latest demonic attack on God's people, so I will say no more at this time; we have plenty of articles on it. To put it plainly, every 'big' issue has been put upon me strongly by God, even though at times I might feel anxious and unable.

I have learned to just do what God says, and leave the results to Him! I do not yet know if God will give me another 'huge' topic to tackle, but this shows that my friend, Peter, got it wrong... I did not chase something to write about, God just put each subject into my head and heart, whether or not I wanted it!

So, the early demand was for us to leave the system of churches. This we did and examined everything before we implemented it, as directed by God Himself in scripture. We have all agreed – none of us can ever return to the mainstream system of churches. I should add that fellow members made this conscious decision before I even mentioned it. In no way do I attempt to cajole them to follow me. And when I leave this earth, someone else will take on the pastoral role. I can only pray that they will not reverse on their decisions and beliefs.

Today, there is more 'movement' as I follow scripture in the matter of the pastorate, as I again try to adhere to the biblical model even moreso. Though I have been close to it for over 30 years, I now have to take it to the logical biblical conclusion. And, our meetings tend to follow that same pattern. In particular I refer to 'redoing' the vital but lowly role of pastor.

Also, members are aware (because of my age) that another pastor or pastors need to be elected by God, for when I am no longer here. Again, according to scripture. They do not 'need' such elders to function – God will always guide them no matter who is part of the membership, or if there are pastors!

It is fair to say that our gathering of ekklesia* is dynamic, because it speaks to each other as well as to and from God. The spirit of each meeting is, to us, as it was during the formation of the earliest churches. No, we do not wish to go backwards, or to resurrect the first century gatherings. But, the spirit of the meetings, hopefully, is the same... open, Christocentric, true to God's word and to each other.

Nothing is hidden, and nothing is avoided because it seems 'too hard'. We urge all local churches to abandon their traditionalism in favour of 'freedom in Christ'. (See Galatians 2 etc). Only the "false brethren" wish to be rid of this freedom! Today, many such false brethren fill churches. Few operate as they should, and most follow the rigidity of traditionalism.

(*Reminder – the Greek word 'ekklesia' does not intrinsically mean 'saved people' only. What makes it refer to saved people is the context, which qualifies the word in each case as God's people. Used in other historical texts, it can have one of several other meanings. Some make much of its use, instead of 'church', but such arguments are irrelevant, because the Bible texts show its meaning in each verse through provision of a suitable context).

Government of Churches

Local churches can operate in many different ways. So long as they adhere to God and His word they cannot go wrong. Or, if they sometimes err, they can repent and change. However, note this:

> *"For unto us a child is born, unto us a son*
> *is given: and the government shall be*
> *upon his shoulder: and his name shall be*
> *called Wonderful, Counsellor, The mighty*
> *God, The everlasting Father, The Prince*
> *of Peace."* (Isaiah 9:6)

A very familiar text. Note that the government will be on HIS shoulder, not ours! That is, the *miśrâ* is His, not ours. 'Government' refers to His rule or dominion. All and any sub-rules are given to mankind to use wisely and according to HIS design and commands. So, any local 'rule' by all of those in a local church is to be under His dominion, not that of a pastor who wishes to 'do his own thing'. This is exemplified in

Isaiah 22:21, where the word for local 'government' is *memšālâ*. In this text it speaks of human rule, which must be made subject to <u>God's</u> rule.

Those who refuse proper godly government in their churches are 'Presumptuous, self-willed and speak evil of those who are held in good esteem.' (2 Peter 2:10).

We see in 1 Corinthians 15:5 that there are "differences of administrations" BUT THE SAME LORD. Do you think each church can do whatever it wishes without deference to the Lord's will or to commands? This does NOT refer to an administrator separate from proper rule. The word for 'administrations' gives the clue – *diakonia*. It speaks of the work of deacons, who assist members in daily tasks, leaving the pastor to do his spiritual tasks.

It does NOT refer to political scheming or office control! So, whilst each local church is free to 'do church' in its own way, it is NOT free to ignore what God establishes, or to follow traditionalism.

Chapter 3

Precept on Precept

"For precept must be upon precept, precept upon precept; line upon line, line upon line; here a little, and there a little:" (Isaiah 28:10)

As a pastor and teacher I had to learn the hard way, bit at a time, and perhaps occasionally in big 'loads'. This is how most so-called 'lay' preachers conduct their ministries (and why they might do so badly). Conversely, men who attend a Bible college and come out with a polished new title of 'Reverend' get it all in one fell swoop! Or, so they fondly think. It took me a lot longer, because I had to find solutions myself. Eventually, I was able to find the right path, thanks to the Lord. Those around me in my local church had no thought for myself or God's demands.

So, who learns the most, and who learns the most useful material? Almost automatically, folks will say the 'trained' person. But, we need more clarification. For example, WHAT did the Bible college person learn? Colleges range from weak and worthless to high-flying and academically brilliant. But, an academic background is not the arbiter. Indeed, nothing like it is found in scripture. God's truths were passed around by letter and by visit. No-one was specially taught by outside agencies.

In my earlier days as a Christian, still in my early twenties, I attempted to get into three Bible colleges, all well-known. Each one advised me against it, so I didn't get in. Frankly, at that time, they were right to reject my applications. I wanted a fast-track biblical education, and it was the wrong motive. Many who become students get this fast-tracking, and gain academically. But, does this make them suitable pastors or preachers?

I gained academically by taking secular degrees plus a theological degree, and by very hard work and study. I then applied these to my biblical research, and so the result is the same. But, did this make me better? I don't think so. What matters is that God calls you to the task at hand, and you live righteously. I sometimes failed in the latter. Once <u>God</u> calls a man to a ministry, He will give him gifts and abilities to enable him to do it right. No Bible college can do that! They can only give extended studies in interesting topics… but, it does not necessarily mean the topics are of God, or are of genuine use.

After my rejections I could see that the colleges were right not to accept me. My biblical understanding was 'all over the place' because, like most, I picked up bits and pieces of theology (well, populist Bible ideas) and did not really know what I was doing. A few examples of this random nature of most

Christian lives is found in my book 'Patchwork Quilt Theology'. The reason I can talk with authority about all this, is that I lived through the same experiences until the Lord guided me out of the darkness and into His marvellous light.

1. A man is elected in eternity
2. He is saved at a specific time in his history
3. He is called by God to preach, teach, etc
4. He is given gifts and ability by God to enable his calling
5. He is called by the Holy Spirit to start ministry
6. What he says and does is from the Spirit
7. His spirit concurs with the Holy Spirit
8. He is 'successful' only when Spirit and spirit coincide
9. Anything else is human folly and uncalled

It took that eureka moment in the Adullam cave text to bring this nonsense to a close. After that, I started to learn in earnest and my pseudo-reformed ideas fell away. It began by understanding that the original languages produced words, and those words had particular meanings. And those meanings were the basis for spiritual interpretation. Our personal ideas about how to interpret a text are irrelevant! And there can be only ONE true interpretation, no matter what words we use.

Then, something far more important arose... the second revelation, that it was the Holy Spirit Who gave accurate interpretation. I use the word 'revelation' to mean a sudden realisation, given by God, that stopped me pretending to be a genuine preacher. I no longer preached, mainly because churches saw my change and did not ask me back! They wanted 'feel-good' sermons, not the authentic word of God. And many paid-pastors are good at discerning things they can, and cannot, teach if they wish to avoid controversy and having their income stopped. (As I discovered, some things I teach are controversial, not because of scripture or myself, but because many refuse the truth when it gets 'gritty' and demanding).

After this, my preaching (when it arose at all) was dynamic. I didn't make it up, I didn't use jokes, and I didn't search for great sounding stories or human interpretations. Nor did I foolishly copy other preachers. I simply prayed, had my text, studied their meanings to get my interpretation, and spoke. Almost without fail, God added His spiritual application and, each time, someone I preached to told me the message was just for them.

I knew when my own soul was interfering and would immediately stop and regain what God wished me to say. And when I did this, the words spoken were powerful. Not because I had written a great sermon, but because I didn't (I no longer preach 'sermons'). Though I had notes, I hardly used them, as the flow of words came to my lips. And every bit of it was biblical, not of myself. (No, I did not become charismatic!). It is all given by God.

In one church (which later asked me to become pastor), as I have said elsewhere, I began preaching from my notes. After about quarter of an hour, I suddenly stopped and put my notes away – I felt strongly prompted by God to do so. I then began to preach as the words came, such was the strength or compulsion from the Holy Spirit. Within minutes many began to cry as God moved their hearts. Then, the doors and windows, on a quiet day, began to rattle loudly, causing more weeping. I carried on in like manner until the end of the speaking time, though I did not check on my watch. Why did the rattling occur? I can only guess.

In another case, I was asked to speak at Arthur Harris' church one evening. I spoke on the reality of the Holy Spirit and how Christians can know real dynamic faith. The meeting finished at about 8pm and we had the usual tea and cakes. I assisted to wash up, and all the while members were clustering around me asking many questions. Not just one or two, but everyone present. They were so excited by the truth (even though Arthur was also teaching truth), they would not stop their queries. We finally got away after midnight!!

Some years later, I was asked to speak at a seaside village (Mumbles) outside the main city (Swansea), a spot frequented by tourists. This was after the morning meeting in the church I then attended, in mid-afternoon on a sunny day. I stood on the stage that was set up on the grass and church members all sat around in the park. The place was filled with visitors to the village, all milling around. They were not taking any notice of those peculiar people singing hymns... they often came across outdoor preachers in their home towns, and ignored those, too.

I held the microphone and spoke without notes or predetermined words. As I spoke, I felt the words suddenly take on their own power, so I knew this was going to be a vital message from God. Quickly, the visitors who were passing by stood still, and everyone listened. The one who had asked me to speak came up to me later and was very excited. He spoke of the impact the preaching had had on visitors and members alike, and said that God had told him I would become a great outdoor speaker. My reply might sound strange, but I said "The problem is, God has not told ME that". So, I never spoke at those meetings again. The man's excitement was not the issue. Unless GOD commanded me to speak again, I would not do it. This criterion should be known by every speaker at every meeting.

Bit by bit, I was learning when to speak, what to say, and how to listen to the Spirit within. Everything else is man-made. Yes, I could have continued being a 'star' speaker outdoors, and this would have made me more than acceptable to those who were members, but I had the immediate witness in my spirit that the 'offer' was not right for me. Soon after that I took up the ministry (BTM) given to me by God, and the pastorate, after leaving the 'system'.

Precepts...

Do not think I am dismissive of Bible college men, or the whole of the 'system'. I am not. The journey I took was my own. It was how God led me. How He leads others is not my concern – it is up to Him. There are very good men in pastorates today who are products of Bible colleges. And there are very good folks who listen to them in their own churches. But, for me, and others, it was not how God worked.

For myself, I had to learn "precept upon precept". Bit at a time. That it caused me to move away from the 'system' is something that still amazes me… though it dismayed those who observed! If we move a little farther from that text, we have this: "…this is the refreshing: yet they would not hear". That is a sad fact. When we moved out of the 'system' (of traditionalist churches) we were shunned. Yet, those who did this knew nothing about us. Obviously, there is a lot more behind this period. Were we right? I can only say we acted as we did because God led us out. There is no point in raking over old problems. Suffice to say the 'proof is in the pudding', as we grew from strength to strength in our spiritual lives.

Interestingly, verse 13 seems prophetic of charismatic debauchery: "*… that they might go, and fall backward, and be broken, and snared, and taken*". It is interesting because this was the big topic I was led to tackle after dealing with the AIDS scandal. It arose out of the way the UK was deluded enough to follow the Toronto Blessing. When I was first told about it my spirit immediately said it was a fake movement and was not of the Holy Spirit. After this I studied what was happening around the world and amassed much information, which all proved my 'intuition' was correct. None of the 'Blessing' was biblical. The result of this was more shunning, by those who were deluded by it!

Nevertheless, following God and not Man can bring much grief to one who is called to a different action. It immediately brands you as a freak, a backslider, a brutish unbeliever. The insults and shunning were the price we had to pay to follow the Lord and not the 'system'. It initially hurt, but it was essential.

At the same time, we were all taught, precept upon precept. In the Hebrew this means to listen to, and act upon, a command or ordinance (of God). (Note: others suggest the term is mocking Isaiah. This is a theological opinion and not a proven fact).

This is how true learning takes place – bit at a time. If someone is taught in 'crash' fashion, all in one go, little is retained. To truly learn we must be taught something basic, and then build upon it in small units until we really understand: "… here a little, and there a little." Too many today have much knowledge but little understanding, with no experience in using it.

Now, about 55 years after I first began to teach scripture, I follow the same principles. I will introduce a doctrinal command and explain it. At another time,

I will do the same again, but from a different text. And so we build up knowledge. By encouraging questions and comments, doctrine is reinforced and properly understood. As a teacher/lecturer I always told students that the proof they really knew a subject was when they could repeat it in their own words. By doing so they showed that they had assimilated facts and could use them in suitable contexts.

I can tell when someone has this secure knowledge by the way they speak. Merely repeating Bible verses does not cut it! Even Satan knows the Bible, inside out! When we KNOW scripture we can repeat it, not by quoting verses alone, but by using the concepts behind them. It is this that we practice in our meetings. Few Christians relish the thought of having to do this, because it shows up their lack. Yet, we ALL lack to some degree, and this is why our members are not embarrassed to admit lack of knowledge. We learn from each other!

I do not say this out of superiority, but out of memory… it is how I was years ago! Any inadequacy I identify in others is also present in me. It took me many years to come away from the 'system' – how local churches act and speak. So, I completely understand how others are caught up in such a false environment. I had to learn bit at a time, precept upon precept. In this book I try to speed-up the transition from self to godly motivation, by illustrating the steps we took in our own church. Why waste time searching for answers or reinventing the wheel!

Though I understand how this wrong activity happens, it also saddens me greatly that fellow believers have not really moved from the point of salvation and are unwilling to learn truth when outside their pews! Many can quote Bible verses and popular explanations, but how many study what they read in scripture, and listen to the Spirit teaching them inwardly, and apply those scriptures with genuine knowledge and understanding? Yes, many can do so with divine authority – but many more cannot. Hence the bad state churches are in today.

I speak with concern, not with pride. Oh how easy it is to sit in a pew, shake hands at the door, and forget. That is not Christian living, it is a false environment where stasis is the rule, not genuine dynamic movement of the spirit, which guides the soul. (It is evident that the two are separate).

I have lost count of the Christians who contact me asking what they should do – they love the Lord but their churches show a distinct lack of knowledge and real Christian faith. And some even have bad behaviour, such as heavy shepherding, separation of 'minister' and 'laity', plus poor biblical teaching. In short, 'church life' is predictable and boring as mud. So, the need is there, and in abundance.

I have travelled a long distance to speak at churches, without recompense . I have taken meetings in small churches that only spoke Welsh (though I could only read Welsh and sing it). I have spoken in remote villages in rural England. I have (with James, my brother-in-law) taken a weekend of Creation v Evolution in a church with attendees who were scientists. I have spoken in a back store-room which contained spare pews and listeners had to twist around to hear me, using only a dim light. I have sung the Gospel many times in small gatherings, and even in a choir in England. I have spoken to young people in homes, where they were eager to learn about the spiritual realm. And I have preached with a line of elders sitting behind me, their eyes boring through the back of my neck! In other words I have preached and taught in many places, and when I spoke with Holy Spirit prompting there were lovely responses I never had when I tried to copy my peers! And I was even invited to become an elder in a huge Apostolic church! (Very odd).

What I am saying is that preaching according to popular demand gets us nowhere. Preaching from the heart, with a mind led by the Spirit, is very different. The past 35 years in particular have been full of amazing features. I have been led by God from one vital subject to another. How do I know they are from God and not my own imagination?

Mainly, those subjects have caused me sometimes intense grief. No-one likes to be 'out in the cold' and few deliberately set out to invite trouble to their door. Each subject I have tackled (under my BTM ministry) has been confrontational, not because I ask for it, but because the subject matter demands it, and God prompts me to speak out. By following God's prompting I have even lost my job. And in theological issues I have not gained many friends, but mainly enemies. Yet, I am no rebel, nor do I intentionally seek out issues that cause me grief. They just happen. Why does this not happen to others? Because they refuse to speak out when it is necessary. But, a quiet life is not necessarily a godly one. And most rarely hear of people like me.

I must add that during the past decades of teaching etc., my wife was with me fully. Not once did she call on me to stop or to stay silent. She understood what was at stake – God's truth; and she often said my ministry was more important than anything else, though she suffered alongside me and even when we both lost our jobs because of wicked homosexuals. For this I was extremely grateful. Her contribution to my ministry will always be remembered. I say this with Job's antithetical wife in mind: she urged Job to curse God so that He would strike Job down. In this way, she argued, he would at least not suffer anymore! What a delusion.

It is important when a man enters into ministry of any kind, that his wife is with him all the way. If his wife is not fully intent on supporting her husband, the ministry will suffer, whether or not he is Bible college trained. And she must not only support him, she must fully understand what God does through him. If not, she will not understand why she makes so many sacrifices.

For the 35 years since my publishing ministry began, I worked full time in responsible jobs, and worked on ministry matters before going to work and when I returned home, and on days off. Any man who thinks 'ministry' is done between 9 and 5 is already lost in his own traditionalism. During the period (several years) I fought against charismatic devilry (because it even attempted to enter our own church), I worked far into the early morning after work and before I went to work, and yet the Lord made sure I retained strength and vigour. Bear in mind that during that week I also had to prepare for Sunday meetings and counsel members and others, so I rarely had time off. Many who think their pastorate is called by God have plenty of time off and never work 'extra'. As far as I am concerned my ministry is full time and more... and this is how it has been for a very long time.

I studied theologically for many decades, including Greek and Hebrew (the latter to a lesser degree because I had to look after my wife), and no longer rely on others (such as commentaries, etc). This is because my ministry is mine alone. I am fully and only responsible. I was called to it by God, and only He can remove me. I do not accept the nonsense about 'laity'... I am just as called as any man who attended Bible college. I have similar knowledge (if not more at times) and I can apply it, again with God's mercy and grace. I am only His vessel, a conduit through which He speaks. In myself, I am nobody, and that is what I prefer. So – no Rolex watch or white suits!

There is no such thing as 'laity' and 'priest'! It is a device used by traditionalists who want control over others, or who want to be put on a pedestal. And, many of this kind want more than the satisfaction of knowing they are doing His bidding. They also like the money, assumed power, and status. They usually start off small and apply for bigger churches as they go along… because they pay more and their star grows brighter! Apart from anything else, scripture does not speak of itinerant pastors who treat the pastorate as a career rather than as a calling from God to be a lowly under-shepherd.

It is no coincidence that this attitude is reflected in job applications etc. When employers want referees they will accept someone of note in the community – a doctor, a police officer, or a pastor. This is because they see pastors as equal to other 'professionals'. And so, many pastors see themselves as professionals with a career. This is an ugly distortion of what a pastor really is.

Now you have a rough background we will look at topics of note, that ALL believers should discuss and put right.

Chapter 4

Pastors

I will be introducing readers to topics we, as a church, have studied intensely. You will find many more topics in the Publications' List at the end of the book. Such studies are ongoing because, as the wesbite says, we are "Reformed and reforming". I find it frustrating and sad that so many who say they are 'Reformed' never move from that spot. The Reformers did not die so we could simply sit in their empty chairs and recall their finest moments! They believed and were willing to die for it. Would YOU die for your faith and beliefs? They died after God brought their own souls back to life, a life that Satan hates, after having their consciences alerted by God. Satan moved rulers against them so they were put to death.

Today, many Christians say they are Reformed, but that is where they are stuck. The Reformers only BEGAN a change; they expected others to continue with it. Yet, how many tracts given out in the streets talk about the Reformers and those with true faith who lived centuries ago? How many sermons talk about the same faithful men and women of long ago? Where are examples from today? It is people of today who the unsaved are interested in; the Reformers and other 'ancients' can be discussed with fellow believers. But, trying to convince the unsaved with stories of people they know nothing about is counter-productive.

It is pointless to say we are Reformed when Rome is again the 'ruling party' (along with lap-dog Anglicanism) and the West is crammed to the sky with heresies and cults! We must <u>keep</u> reforming, daily. Not just as an antidote to Romanism, but also to traditionalism and cultic beliefs. This is ongoing and urgent, but how many heed the call?

When the Reformers famously and bravely gave their lives, pastorates were usually held by Anglican priests. There were a few who were not a part of this social order and were 'laymen', without education from colleges. Some of these 'laymen' were burnt at the stake just like their Reformer friends, because their words were the same. Yet, in biblical terms there are no 'laymen', only men called by God to a particular ministry. And each of them is a sub-shepherd without his own power or authority base.

Later we had John Bunyan. When he was 16 he joined the Parliamentary Army during the Civil War. Aged 19 he returned to his village and trained as a tinker. He first attended an Anglican church, but soon moved to a non-conformist church before becoming a preacher – untrained of course. But, who dares to question his grasp of scripture and doctrine?

For this reason he was put into prison for 12 years. A while later he became pastor of the same church

– yet he is remembered in the Church of England. He is even praised annually with a 'Lesser Festival', so he is not counted to be THAT significant, though his influence has exceeded that of most Anglicans in any age or Christian population!! Though a 'layman' who worked for his weekly wage at a lowly job, he was exalted by God.

My point is this: people like Bunyan were important figures in the history of the Church, though they were 'untrained' officially. Yet, we only have to read Pilgrim's Progress or The Holy War, to see his spirit was totally of God. Few have a similar standing, though they WERE trained in colleges. For me, the vital factor is not training or no-training, but the condition of the man's soul and spirit*.

*The soul (mind, emotions, thoughts, etc) is alive in any man, saved or not. By contrast, the spirit is only alive in the man who is saved. After salvation the soul is subject to the spirit, and the spirit is subject to the Holy Spirit. If a man is truly called to be a pastor, his soul – thinking, emotions, etc – will be led by his spirit, which itself is led by the Holy Spirit, and all this will be evidenced in his character.

Thus, the man is called by God to pastor in a local church, whether or not he has been trained in a Bible college. The calling to do this is personal, but will be noted by others. That is, the man will already be known to his fellow believers as one with publicly known attributes of soul and spirit. He will show the characteristics found in scripture, where a 'pastor' is also known as a presbyter, or elder, or bishop. The names are all referring to the same person, who is a lowly servant to all.

Because he already shows these marks of a genuine pastor, others will automatically veer toward him <u>as</u> a pastor. Thus, in normal circumstances, a pastor is 'home grown'. There is no biblical support for pastors to place advertisements asking for 'adoption' by local churches, or for travelling around looking for pastorless churches! How many are called by God in their own churches, but refrain from obeying the call because they are afraid? Or, because fellow members think they 'must' call a Bible-college-trained 'Reverend'?

In the dim and distant past I remember one man paying an American company so he could use the title 'Reverend'. He then hawked this around, actually sending letters to churches asking for them to invite him to speak. He did this for many years, though his 'sermons' were nothing but garbage and he 'spoke' through puppets! And he further profited by asking for preaching fees, getting free holidays, and otherwise defaming the glorious name of the Lord with his wickedness. *(Out of curiosity, I found the company he used and applied for a reverend-ship. For a few pounds I received a certificate and confirmation that I was indeed Reverend Napier and an associate preacher of a dud church denomination! What a farce!).*

I know the man was a complete fraud, yet what is the difference if a genuine Christian attends a genuine Bible school and similarly looks around for a pastorate, or places advertisements looking for one? Why do local churches search frantically for a pastor, when such a man might be already amongst their own membership? God does not leave earnest believers on their own for long!

Pastorship is not a career, so why do so many think it is? They show their belief in being a 'professional' by moving around in a variety of pastorships, usually gradually climbing the socio-spiritual ladder to 'higher' callings until they reach a famed church. In this way many would-be 'big names' will take on a poor church to begin with, until they can reach their desired goal of a big-name church. So, the 'lower' status church is only a stepping-stone… what a gross insult!

There can be bad consequences in doing this. How many pastors move around so much, their wives become sad victims of their itchy-feet? I once nursed one such wife, a very sad 'case'. She became morose and depressed, because she never stayed long enough in one place to have friends or a settled life. This led to a hospital admission after she displayed the symptoms of Bi-Polar (then known as manic-depression). Is this caused by a wife's genuine distress, or by a man trying to be a pastor against all inner testimony? Is his 'calling' REALLY of God, if his wife suffers badly?

Once in a hospital such folks will usually confide in staff looking after them. She told of her intense sadness, because while her husband moved to the locality for what he might have called legitimate reasons and a 'call from God' (was it, given the results?), she was left stranded once again, without friends or purpose. In spite of having Christian responses and help (from myself) the husband did not take it seriously, and his wife one day simply walked into the sea and drowned herself. How many poor wives of pastors are in a similar bad position? Sadly, everyone think a pastor's wife is an extension of a pastor! No, she is not. She is a person in her own right, and her calling may not coincide with that of a selfish husband.

I knew others, even younger people, who were caught in an unreal world of 'Christian' life, where they followed all the right actions, and said the right things, but whose churches had no idea how to deal with them. Pastors are supposed to offer this kind of guidance. It is what they are there for, and why they are called 'pastors'.

It is usual that pastors who are paid are required to preach or teach Bible twice or three times on Sundays, and also at other times during the week. Frankly, this is a relentless and frantic way to live. It is my view that the pastor must act as he is called to do so by the Holy Spirit. He must be "apt to teach", but he should NOT be thought of as a sermon-cruncher! Just one 'sermon' can sometimes take all week. To be expected to churn out maybe half a dozen a week is almost tyrannical! Sometimes, the pastor can manage more IF he is called by God to do so. But, if he only churns them out because it is expected of him, he will soon 'burn out' and collapse, as many have, some with dire consequences.

Let GOD lead the man to teach or preach, NOT the congregation, just because they pay him. And remember, on top of all that he is expected to visit the sick (biblically, this is the province mainly of the deacons) and preach in other churches or at conferences. THESE ARE NOT his prime goals given by God; they are human desires.

"Apt to teach" is one word in Greek – *didaktikos*. It means he is given a gift from God to teach well. How else can he properly guide the sheep in Christ's fold? It is not a natural ability, though some may indeed have a natural talent for study and speaking. It is far more: it means that when he has to guide others the Lord will give him what to say and think. If he uses Bible college units to guide, he will not be doing what he should. Every person is different, so there can be no 'one size fits all'!

Even worse is if he takes a counselling course and uses that as an approach. (My MA dissertation examined NHS psychology/counselling and Bible-based Christian counselling. Unfortunately, I discovered that both were identical. Which means 'counsellors' are taught pseudo-psychology based mainly on secular theories. Psycho-babble).

Being apt to teach does NOT mean the pastor (see below) must do all the preaching and teaching, only that when he does so he will be good at it (because the Holy Spirit guides him before he guides the members). Others may speak, so long as they are called by God to do so.

I first preached about a year after being saved. I remember it well, because it was 1966, in the week of the Aberfan disaster in Wales, when a coal tip slid down a hill and engulfed the local school, killing many children and adults. I referred to it in my preaching. Much later I realised I was asked to preach far too soon after salvation, probably as a novelty. In many ways, though I was learning fast, I was like the blind leading the blind and in reality I was not equipped to speak. And this continued for twenty years! (Until my 'revelation' about king Saul).

During those twenty years I dutifully wore a suit and tie to meetings and when speaking. I was a little more casual when singing with my mother, who sang with me and played piano, while I played guitar. So, I maintained the 'proper' image so required by my peers... which reminds me of the same silliness I came across one hot summer's day...

On a day off work, I was wearing a flimsy cotton Tee shirt and shorts. It was very hot and as I was driving (to where I cannot remember) I caught sight of my then pastor sitting outside the church. I stopped and decided to have a quick chat, just as company. When I reached him, he was wearing a suit, the jacket on the back of a chair, and a tie.

I couldn't believe this ridiculous adherence to peer-required dress! Concerned, I said it was alright to unbutton the top of his shirt and undo his tie, if not remove it! I added that it was okay in the heat to roll up his sleeves. He was visibly sweating profusely. He rolled his sleeves up and that was that. I just could not believe his unnecessary suffering! But, that is what he was taught in Bible college and what peers expected of him.

Today, if called to speak, I would not wear a suit and tie, even if I had them! Do you think the Apostles wore formal attire when travelling between churches and preaching? Today, many preachers do so because it is expected of them as 'professionals'.

Titles
Remember, 'pastor' is not a title. Some think it is a mark of humility to be called 'pastor' instead of 'reverend'. Really, it is just as auspicious a title! The word 'pastor' is only found once in the whole of the KJAV, Jeremiah 17:16. The English comes from the Hebrew, *rā'â*. It means to be an herdsman or shepherd, a companion, a teacher, a special friend. Interestingly, it can also mean an idolater. Should not a pastor be a special friend to his fellow believers?

Even though he does not get a special title, or colourful ribbons and medals to denote his service?

A pastor should have a special bond with his fellow members, so that he notices needs and will step in when asked to deal with something spiritual, freely. It should be noted that in the New Testament a pastor should be one of several, especially in larger gatherings. He should not be 'the' pastor, but 'a' pastor... just one sub-shepherd amongst others, each equal to each other, a servant of all.

Today, we have a not-so-subtle hierarchy throughout almost all churches. It is headed by a single pastor, who presides over so-called 'elders', who are 'higher' than the deacons. The deacons tend to be selected by church members, and under them comes the congregation, Sunday School teachers, etc., and others of lowly character. Deacons tend to put their names forward to become elders. None of this is scriptural!

Where churches do have other pastors, they, too, are part of an hierarchy – the 'main' or senior pastor; below him may be an 'assistant pastor'' or several, and others below them with 'official titles'. Usually the pastor who has not been to Bible college is called a 'teaching elder', but NOT a 'pastor'. The variations change according to denomination or church. And it is all unbiblical. A pastor is an elder is a presbyter is a bishop! All names for the same person. And none of them is a title. Once a man has a title, he becomes an 'official' or an 'officer'. There are none in the Bible.

A pastor (singular or several) is just a Christian who has been gifted and called to guide the local flock as a sub-shepherd. He is not free to do as he wishes, but must always teach what Christ would teach (as found in scripture). He is not a leader or a manager or the boss of a local church. He is there to look after everyone and to help them live as fellow believers, watching over their spiritual safety. How different from the majority of modern churches, especially those 'mega-churches' with an army of proud titles and 'officers', paid to be 'professional'.

In my own life I have two separate but linked roles – Bible teacher and pastor. When we meet on Sundays I teach scripture. This is separate from being a pastor – a role that may not be seen in every meeting, but only when someone requires guidance.

Carefulness
A pastor is always a male. This is because that is given to us in the New Testament. Being male, he should be extra-careful not to give counsel to lone females. I have known many otherwise good men fall to this error, damaging their souls and lives, and leading to divorce. I can assure pastors that Satan loves to meddle and destroy the witness of pastors, by simply urging them to counsel females alone. In one year a few decades ago, I witnessed SIX well-

known pastors fall to this folly of post-counsel sexual impropriety. It happens all too often.

ALWAYS be accompanied by a wife or some other female who will not spread gossip about any advice given. The same applies if, rarely, an homosexual asks for counsel. The potential dangers are real. Sometimes this can be put aside if the female is one of his own family, though it is usually a good idea to have a female Christian with a pastor if he counsels a female, if only to add feminine comfort when needed.

And when giving counsel, a pastor should not allow the 'session' to carry on for hours! Keep the visit short, maybe no more than an hour. There are very good reasons for this. For example, if allowed an unlimited time, the discussion will just carry on, becoming unstructured and aimless.

Keep to the point. God will show the pastor if there is a need to move away from the main point in order to clarify something. By making the 'session' short it helps the counsellee to maintain what is important, and not to wander without aim into unessential areas, just chatting!

Other sessions can always be allowed but only as directed by God. And, importantly, any counsel must be directive. That is, with purpose and with an expectation that the counsellee will show results (e.g. stop sinning, repent, apologise to others who are hurt, and so on). There is absolutely no point whatever in just talking forever with no goal, or repeating matters already talked about. In God's mind any counsel must always be consistent with scripture, always relevant, and always require a biblical response. And without formal counselling 'training' and certificates!

When working with psychiatric patients I noted that most loved to talk forever with a therapist/nurse about their supposed maladies. But, they are less prone to do anything that changes their 'mental' state. This is because they prefer to 'suffer' than to take steps towards responsibility. Many Christians are the same, as they comfortably encompass sin.

How Much Work?
Whether paid or not a pastor must work according to what God demands of him. He is not the plaything of members or deacons, etc., and should not be told what to do by them (unless he has erred). So long as he is following the Lord His time should be spent in the matters he has been called to deal with by God – primarily, guiding the local flock. Secondarily, this will also mean knowing his scripture and applying it to those he helps. He may, or may not, speak at every meeting.

Being a pastor does not necessarily mean he leads the local church, or that he must administer communion. (Communion is to be shared, not governed or 'administered'. See later section).

Remember – a pastor is just one member of several or many. He is not greater or more important than anyone else. Obviously, he must show adherence to scripture and use it with skill – God gives this skill. And if he is faithful, other members must give him due honour.

Like anyone else, a pastor must have proper rest periods. To expect him to teach or preach half a dozen times a week is not good. He needs time to pray, to study scripture, and to prepare what he has to say. And, of course, he must have time to counsel members. Could be once a week or less. His working week should not be up to members or deacons, but according to what God calls him to do. Again, I repeat – no woman may be a pastor.

Other Tasks

It is strange that many pastors take time off from their own churches to speak often in others, especially if those other places are foreign. By all means use such a time to also have a holiday, but no pastor has a role to play in other churches, unless his local role has been fulfilled.

In my own life I give counsel whenever needed, prepare for Sunday studies, and also stay committed to the ministry given by God (BTM). It is a very full schedule, but I start and stop when needed, and as God leads. Because I am also a pastor taking Sunday meetings my 'work' load is seven days a week. If I take time off it is usually on weekdays so as I can still be here for Sundays. In essence, then, I do far more 'work' than many paid pastors.

How many hours a pastor performs his role is up to himself and God. No congregation should force him into more and more work. When both congregation and pastors work together in joy, there should be no problems.

There are times, too, when a pastor needs to simply do nothing. I noticed my own 'rest period' over the Christmas period as I proof-read this book, but it wasn't just a 'rest'. I simply did very little – it was the first Christmas in 55 years that I did not share it with my wife. Over the period I felt empty and it seemed God did not prompt me to continue my ministry for a few days, though certain serious counselling had to take place during my own remembrance of my wife. It never stops, but perhaps members and readers can bear in mind that a pastor needs loving support, too! His role does not end for feast days!

There is much more I could say. For example, though I might teach truth, some will not obey God. This is then their problem, not mine, if I have given godly counsel. This can be in my role as pastor, or as someone with an extra ministry, such as BTM.

Obviously, if the problem is sin, then I must demand, in God's Name and according to His word, that the sin is stopped and repented of. The same demand is made of myself. But, few people who sin like to be told this. I have come across many in all my years who appear to listen and obey God, but whose inward desires are very different. Some even become worse in their sins.

This is not in the province of a pastor. If he guides as per scripture and the sinner does not listen, well, the onus is on him or her to repent, stop, and move along the true path of righteousness. The pastor cannot force compliance with truth and holiness! If he has done whatever God wants him to do and has counselled wisely, the responsibility passes on to the one who continues to sin. If that sin is serious enough, it might lead to casting out of fellowship, even if the person involved is a family member. In these cases our emotions are irrelevant; what matter is God's commands.

(For more, see the book, 'Will the Real Pastor Please Stand Up?' BTM/Petra Press).

Chapter 5

Meetings

When talking about any section of this book, remember I am giving the reader what we as a local church do. Just as I had to learn precept upon precept, so all of us did the same thing when it comes to meetings.

You may, or may not, adopt similar ways to meet. You must agree spiritually with the Holy Spirit, not just with me. All I am doing is passing-on what WE did, and continue to do. Indeed, it might even change once I am taken from this world. Then, those who are left must ask God if they are to continue, or not. This is because no current church is the same as the church when it was opened. Only current faith is counted, not the past.

After we left the 'system', as with every other aspect of our Christian lives, we all searched scripture and applied what we knew to be truth to what we do. And so we looked at how to have meetings together. We also looked at that peculiar hybrid known as 'worship' meetings. (See my article on this). A very muddled concept and very far from what God says, even in Reformed' churches!

The very first thing is to examine scripture, and the most major aspect is very simple:

"For where two or three are gathered together in my name, there am I in the midst of them." (Matthew 18:20)

In the days after Christ returned to Heaven, meetings took place mainly in houses of believers. Some met in fields, especially when Rome took umbrage at them after being fed lies by angry Jews, who often led others against Christians. Some even met in tolerant synagogues because of the Old Testament content of meetings, until the Jews became irate and told them to leave. And very close to the ascension of Christ, some even attended the Temple. This, however, does not give us an excuse to meet as we wish, with whomever we wish.

The Matthew text was uttered by Christ Himself, so must be taken as an imperative. The text, with verse 19, says that Christ will always be in the midst of a meeting of Christians, because even if there are only two, they constitute a meeting of the true ekklesia (the church in that place). This should make every believer think twice about what they call a 'meeting', especially when modern meetings are cast in stone and are incapable of real spiritual life.

If Christ is with even two Christians wherever they meet, then that is a 'church meeting', because a 'meeting' is not about a place, a building, or even a scheduled gathering. It is about at least two people who are saved being together, for ANY good purpose. Even as they chat about daily things, they are the church in that place at that time!

This means that when I meet another Christian in a supermarket, Christ is with us, and we have a 'meeting'. We have a meeting if we gather to discuss business. Or, if we attend a sporting event. Or, if we see each other on holiday or on a day out. Or, if we gather more formally on a Sunday or any other day. If the two are both saved by grace and faith alone, Christ is in that meeting.

This has big ramifications for what a true meeting is. Firstly, it shows that gathering formally in a building (normally awkwardly called a 'church') MUST contain ONLY saved people to enable it to be called a meeting with Christ present. Others, unsaved, may attend, but they are outside this definition of a Christ-involved meeting. Such a meeting is for the saved only, because Christ is not with the unsaved (though He might bring their spirits alive – born again – or stir their consciences. This, however, is incidental).

In our meetings we have regularly had unsaved folks sitting in with us. yet, the meeting is for the saved. If the unsaved are touched by anything they are free to speak, but the meeting itself is only for the saved.

(Note: We have had unsaved people in our meetings, and a rare few have been the cause of much heartache and trouble. Be careful who you allow to sit-in on meetings. It is not virtuous or godly

to allow them to attend if they show signs of trouble and mayhem).

This means that when local meetings always have an evening service just for the unsaved, they are not godly devices. Such meetings are not in accordance with Matthew 18:20, but they are something else. Indeed, they enter the province of the evangelist. An evangelist' role is for the unsaved, often in an unsaved environment. Whereas, the meeting of the church is just that – a meeting for and with the saved. Attendance by the unsaved is incidental, and in a meeting of the true ekklesia all effort and time is spent on the saved in that place.

There have been times when I have been invited to a meal, for example, and have been asked specifically to raise a topic on salvation for fellow attendees who are unsaved! I eat my meal and sit with everyone. But, I only speak on salvation if the topic arises 'naturally' (because God provides an opportunity). If it is forced upon everyone by an unsubtle 'hint', I refuse to join in. Unless the Lord prompts me to speak I won't.

Sundays
Meetings have been held for years on a Sunday because it is the only day most members can attend. As a nurse, for example, I was forced to work on Sunday mornings even though when I was employed I asked for the day off so as to hold meetings. But, when an homosexual became my superior, she

demanded I work Sundays, because she hates Christians. So, I worked and then returned home in the afternoon to hold our meetings. Remember what Christ said: that the day of rest was made for mankind – not the other way around! Others might be in employments that allow them to work, such as police, forces, ambulances, nurses, etc. As far as able they should try their best to not work Sundays, but should not be castigated if they cannot avoid it. Others who need not work Sundays do so willingly – I cannot speak for their consciences.

(In actuality, the Lord demands that we take a seventh-day rest. This may, or may not, be a Sunday… but this is not the place to discuss what the sabbath' is for believers. See my articles).

In our Sunday meetings we discuss all kinds of things on the minds of members. This is usually before anything I have to say. The topics are things on the minds and hearts of some present, including particular Bible texts, books read, things that have happened in the week, and so on. We then discuss them until an answer is achieved, if possible, and if one is needed.

At times there are no queries, only comments. We discuss those also. As I recently had to remind our church, I am not the most important member there, and what I have to say does not supersede what every other member wishes to talk about. Remember, I am only one member of many and my role as a pastor is separate from my role as Bible teacher, though on times they both coincide.

Sometimes the matters to hand are of vital importance to all or some of us. So, we spend time on those things. If needed we take time later to study the facts and then continue at another time. It does not matter if children or adults raise queries.

This continues until the matters are either spoken or resolved. If we run out of time, then I will not take part with a Bible study, and will commence the study at the next meeting. On occasions, if everyone agrees, we will still have a Bible study, though it adds a lot of extra time to the meeting. Can you imagine any traditionalist church allowing any of this to happen?

I am a nobody. I am led by God to speak or to pastor, but I am not the 'main man' or the star attraction. We are ALL important before God. So, if time runs out I do not sulk or insist we stay longer! (As I have witnessed in some pastors).

What Do We Do?
Most occasions, we have our run of discussions. Then, if time, I will give the study lesson, which always contains an application to our own lives. Every week, a member or two will say that what is taught exactly suited their current lives or thoughts. This is because the speaker is open to being led by God, and not because he is particularly 'clever' or magically imbibed with 'supernatural' knowledge.

All this time we sit together around the room. When children are with us they are taken into a separate room to be taught by someone who loves to speak to kids. Their meeting is always around and about scripture, in their own language. This might include songs, artwork, simple Bible readings, and so on. Always realise that this meeting is for unsaved children (some are saved at an early age, but that is rare), but the teacher will still speak of scripture and basic 'theology' they can understand, so they are given a basic grounding in morality and reverence for the Lord, even if they are presently unsaved.

It should be noted that the concept of holding Sunday School is not found in scripture. However, the concept of children being taught at their mother's knee is found in God's word. The aim, apart from giving a simple introduction to what salvation is, is just to keep the children employed in something interesting until they are old enough to sit in with the adult meeting. (Which they often do in our meetings). Obviously the teacher will have their eternal souls in mind, but he/she also knows that children cannot take in an adult class until the Lord gives them salvation and a mind mature enough to deal with adult themes.

The Adult Diet
When we first left the 'system' we all agreed that we wanted God's word explained every week. There was also agreement that we would study one book at a time, from start to finish. At times, if chapters are

long or complicated, we split the chapters up into two or even three divisions, each taking up a single meeting. I can assure readers that each book we study has a different 'flow' or 'feel' to it, and this helps members to understand them in a special way.

For this reason, when I finish teaching a book, I say I have to 'cleanse my palate', because the next book will be very different in 'feel'. Thus, I might teach one of the Psalms in between going on to teach the next book requested by members. Or, perhaps one of my articles. This then clears my head of the way I had to approach the previous book, in readiness for the new approach of the next book.

We rarely sing because of the stated need of members to have Bible study, but music or songs can come into it if desired. The children love to sing though! Everything depends on how persons believe God is moving them to speak or comment.

Many 'system' Christians are shocked to learn that we have no group prayers. We came to this conclusion at the very start, when we examined what God says about prayer. We found that we have been commanded by Christ to pray on our own in our own rooms. So, I do not pray before the meeting or after it, unless there is a pressing need to do so; such times are rare. We do pray corporately but ONLY if God has pressed every member to do so. That is, each comes with a specific thing to pray about, on the same day, in the same place, about something that is urgent and has been pressed upon EVERYONE. This, too, is rare, but it happens. On occasions someone might feel the need to pray about something on their hearts. There are no hard-and-fast rules. And many important topics might be discussed, but not on Sunday.

In the past, because we formerly sat under 'sermons', I have taught texts that are topic-centred, but, frankly, these are hard to muster every week. We have found that following a whole book of scripture is far more satisfying and spiritually nutritious than a different reading every week. There are many advantages to this, including enabling members to think methodically and to build up doctrinal knowledge.

Usually, the only time I venture away from a whole-book study is when we reach the end of a book and I need to 'cleanse the palate' of my mind by looking at a topic or a very short book before starting on another book. Usually, the next book is chosen by members together. At times, though we have already studied every New Testament book, for example, we will study a book again, because the last time may have been anything up to twenty or thirty years ago. Each time we revisit a book it is always with a fresh mind and sometimes fresh topics.

After each meeting we have a light meal and cup of tea/coffee, and topics again arise. It is true to say that usually every meeting is alive! And sometimes after a meeting we will all go for a walk somewhere nice, if the weather is with us. We may also meet outside Sunday meetings. We have also undertaken a unique moment of baptising a member in the sea on a lovely hot day! (Before this I baptised 3, or was it 4, in a swimming pool abroad).

At no time do I pretend to be greater than others, or of more value. Because I am not. The 'pastor cult' has never been part of our meetings. Indeed, I encourage members to think for themselves, biblically and truly. This is because I am NOT their 'boss' or super-hero!

Visiting

If visits are necessary, because we are a small church, this is done by everyone. In a bigger church it is the lot of the deacons, so as to free a pastor for spiritual study, etc. I used to be very limited because I was looking after my wife. Now, at the age of 75, I am much slower and less fit. So, visiting is at a minimum. Never do something in the church because you feel forced or pressured to do it!! See the next sub-title.

In my own case, mainly folks come to visit me instead. This is especially as my whole time is usually taken up with writing, Bible-researching, answering emails, preparing for Sundays, and so on. We also, on nice days, meet up and go out for day trips, or even shopping. Really, it just living normally, without pressure or hidden agendas.

So-Called 'Witnessing'

No doubt many readers have been hooked by pastors or deacons to do something they did not wish to do. I remember a number of times I was expected to attend outdoor witnessing. On one occasion, when I attended a local church. I had just finished a long shift at the hospital and was on my way home. I did not appreciate being harangued by fellow members, who had had their day off, or were students.

On another occasion I allowed myself to be roped-into an evening 'witnessing' time. I KNOW that many felt as I did – pressured. We all stood in a grassy area not far from the church and in the vicinity of huge blacks of flats. The pastor gave prayers and encouragement, before we were all sent out to the flats to knock on doors to invite them to attend.

Frankly, I wondered if the pastor had read a book on witnessing, and wanted to 'try it out', or if it was just a way to increase numbers of attendees who would give cash for the church! Very few of us wanted to be there. And some did not finish their 'stint' because the people in the flats were notorious for criminal or anti-social behaviour. Their foul language and anger was rather obvious!

Friends, I was a victim of this pressure for a long time before I finally left the system! Especially when it came to being pressured to attend prayer meetings. NO pastor or deacon can force a Christian to do something he does not wish to do. But, unfortunately, it is common in many local churches. This is why, in our church, I demand nothing unless God first demands it of me. Even then, I merely pass on the message, so to speak. It is up to each member to follow it up or not. Too many members of local churches do things because the pastor or deacons demand it (including attending prayer meetings). If God wishes an individual to do something, He will speak to his heart and mind personally, through the Holy Spirit. Anything else is coercion and so, false.

We must all witness – but only if and when the Spirit speaks to us to do so. Perhaps some things are ignored by Christians because they are nervous or even afraid. We cannot force them to comply, even if scripture requires it of us. The Spirit must firstly speak to that person until he complies out of obedience and a genuine inner desire to do so. otherwise it is false and therefore not authentic or genuine. Remember this!

Communion
We do not hold communion as most other churches do! That is, we have thrown aside traditionalism.

Because we have a light meal after meetings (or, rather, it is all part of the meeting), we usually have communion during that time. We do it this way because we all take part together, and no-one 'leads'. And, in the early church, communion was always part of a light meal anyway. (Because no-one should go just to eat full meals).

No-one prepares a special thing to say. We just give a few words based on the day Christ took His last meal. We certainly don't pretend to be 'more holy' and superficially hushed as folks do in traditionalist churches. (There is usually a loud 'buzz' of people chatting about everything under the sun. Then, when the pastor and deacons emerge from a back room, they all go silent and become ultra-solemn, as if a switch had been pressed. Very unreal if not hypocritical). It is all so wooden and false.

So, our meetings are very different, undertaken, we believe, as the Lord would want it. Some are afraid of being so physically close to each other. Some think everyone knows their mind! Some cannot take the honest study. Others begin to see that our 'take' on doctrine may not be to their liking. And some want to sing hymns. As for members, the numbers go up and down. But, this is not important. What matters is being true to the Lord.

Special Days
Another activity is observing special days. In particular, to do with Easter and Christmas. Both are Roman Catholic in origin, but amended in structure to appear to be Protestant!

Read my books on Christmas to know why our church does not celebrate them. There might be other days, such as harvest Sunday. This can be traced way back to Old Testament times when Israel was mainly an agricultural country and the people obeyed God and thanked Him for everything. Having a special tradition for celebrating the harvest He had providentially provided was natural and suitable, and was required by Jehovah. But, today? In a city or some other non-agricultural setting?

I have nothing against such a celebration, unless it is traditionalistic – performed because it is expected by the hierarchy and not out of a true thankfulness. If it is genuine then it is authentic, but the same cannot be said for Easter and Christmas.

Each local church will have their own traditions, that avoid being traditionalistic. But, once a tradition becomes set in concrete and is done automatically, it is no longer of the Holy Spirit. See the difference?

Chapter 6

Prayer Meetings

Now, many readers will be shocked. This is because we do not have 'prayer meetings' (see book on Prayer Meetings'. BTM/Petra Press, or articles). Again, this was discussed after much study into what the Bible says. One text stood out, and still does. It is a major key to the matter of prayer.

> *"But thou, when thou prayest, enter into thy closet, and when thou hast shut thy door, pray to thy Father which is in secret; and thy Father which seeth in secret shall reward thee openly."* (Matthew 6:6)

I had several decades of attending so-called 'prayer meetings', so I am not speaking without knowledge. Now, I find it strange that those who say they are saved by grace continue to attend 'prayer meetings' that are scheduled, often annually. (This chapter is NOT about the need for prayer, only about the way it is done, against the command of Christ).

Christ was referring to men who stand publicly to pray, so others might hear them. This is exactly what happens when churches hold regular weekly prayer meetings… despite claims to the contrary. Have they all not got 'prayer warriors'? Are they really 'warriors' or just modern Pharisees who elongate their robes?

Christ calls such people "hypocrites", and have you ever noticed that usually the same handful of people pray out-loud every week? And have you ever been embarrassed by the pastor's call for 'everyone' to pray one after the other? Is it not true that by the time it comes to your 'turn', you are compelled to speak but feel everyone else has already covered every topic under the sun? All this proves how false it all is. No pastor had the right to command others to pray!

Isn't it also true that you might not feel led to pray, but do it anyway so as not to have people thinking you are somehow deficient? So, you waffle away for a few minutes and finish red-faced? Friends, I know what it is like and have been through similar moments. Even today, I do not like it when well-meaning Christians suddenly ask me to pray. If I am prompted BY GOD to do so I will pray. I don't need others to call me to pray when I have no leading to do so.

> Prayer is a deeply personal activity, which is why our Lord commanded us to pray alone in our rooms. So, why do so many believers counter this command with their own ideas?

When prayer meetings are scheduled months in advance and is a solid part of a weekday meeting, we know straight away that the 'prayers' will rarely, if ever, be prompted by God. Especially as Christ Himself tells us to pray on our own. God does not 'schedule' prayers every Wednesday night at

7.30PM prompt! By their very nature such 'prayers' are NOT impromptu! And have you noticed how the 'prayer warriors' take over the meeting, speak for ages, and usually pray the same things every week (vain repetition), often with flowery language and perhaps even heated emotions?

If I am ever caught in such a situation, I spend my time wisely and simply pray my own prayers. On most occasions, prayers should not be shared with others, because the subjects are too precious or personal. Let us be honest – some will use information put into prayers against the one who prays. And if you don't pray you will no doubt come to the attention of a pastor or deacon, who will question your faith if you remain silent. And if you do not attend prayer meetings, you will probably be consigned not just to the 'naughty step', but to the realm of outer darkness.

Of course, as with all generalisations, this might not all apply to every church… but it seems every church I know of ignores the command in Matthew. Plenty of excuses, but all are invalid.

Do not think I am denigrating any Christian or church. I am merely speaking truth, and giving a view from my side of the fence, a view I believe to be biblical. I must repeat, each section in this book deals with matters I have personally been involved with over many years, and which have been deeply shared and discussed by members. Prayer meetings were a bugbear to me and many others, but members of traditionalist churches dare not speak out, even 'in love' (the usual name given to a sucker-punch). Some from various countries have written to me saying that when they read my original articles on the subject they felt overwhelming relief, because someone dared to speak out. Like so many, they commented that I said what they had all thought and experienced, but did not dare speak to others about it for fear of consequences. Does that sound even remotely loving or Christ-like, or the atmosphere engendered by true biblical values, when others will not allow honest queries? It is one of the worst symptoms of traditionalism.

Those in our church agree with my view, not because I tell them to think this or that way, but because they can see the faults for themselves, and have even suffered because of them... spiritual dictators usually think they are being kind or honest, when they are, in fact, ready to make you feel humiliated when they feel victorious.

It reminds me of a particular therapy session I once had in a psychiatric hospital. About 20 patients came to a large room. A therapist came to take the session and I was there to assist. The therapist urged those present to do all kinds of activities together, and I joined in.

But, then she called on everyone to take off their shoes and socks, and to pick up a large cushion each. They/we were to dance around in a circle and touch each other with the cushions. That was when I refused. It was just silly and of no value. I objected very quietly to the therapist, but the patients noticed that I sat down and did not remove my shoes and socks. That was when things became tense...

One male patient, an expert in marshal arts, walked up to me and demanded to know why I did not join in. Again quietly, I said that I did not need the session because I was mentally balanced, and it was of no value to me. He became irate and said if I didn't do the exercise he would throw me through a window!

I maintained my calm face and spoke gently, again refusing. He then said that by not complying the exercise was in question and this scared him. In other words, he wanted everyone to join in so he felt better, and not for any therapeutic reason. He calmed down after a while, but the point I am making is that I could easily have done what everyone else was doing just to maintain the peace and be like everyone else.

But, there comes a time in all kinds of situations, that a man or woman MUST stand up for genuine principles and God's commands. When others partake just to appease others or to appear to be the same, it brings about tension in one's own mind and heart, because the spirit is not giving the right messages. These sad experiences are within most who attend traditionalistic churches, all of which tend to say that the "prayer meeting is the hub of church life". No, it isn't. The 'hub' is being true to God. Yet, woe-betide anyone who dares to object or query the existence of prayer meetings! There are usually immediate consequences, and none of them good. For this reason Christians actually fear talking about it in their churches, and attend even though their hearts are not in it (because such meetings are not authentic and genuine).

Mixed Meetings

Why do so many churches hold midweek mixed meetings, part Bible study and part prayer? Is it because so few would otherwise attend? Over the years I have had quite a lot of letters or emails from Christians who have always felt unable to support prayer meetings. They have a profound relief, because someone else has voiced their concerns.

Do these mixed meetings mean anything? No, not really, because the 'prayer' part is invalid. How many churches have examined the prayer meetings they hold so 'religiously'? Yes, I have also had communications that claim the individual has been joyous because of prayer meetings. I cannot reject such claims because I was not there at those meetings. However, it is possible that psychological release, for example, is mistaken for spiritual joy. After all, I come across this psychological 'equivalence' in many other areas of Christian life. The extreme example of this psychological 'release' is often found in charismatic churches, complete with raised arms, glazed eyes, and repetitious exclamations of 'Jesus', etc.

If you look at my book on 'Prayer Meetings' you will find I spent many full-time months researching the subject, plus plenty of scriptural texts and Hebrew/Greek meanings. I concluded that nowhere in scripture do we find any command to have prayer meetings per schedule. Not even in the New Testament. You simply will not find it. Prayers yes, but not prayer <u>meetings</u> as we have them today. Search for yourselves (properly).

Most folks 'interpret' badly, so hold to a different view... but, is their view valid? Remember, no-one has the right to have a personal interpretation (2 Peter 1:20. In this text "prophecy of the scripture" refers to how we read and teach scripture. It stands to reason that any text has only ONE interpretation, and it is up to individuals to find and use it. And the interpretation MUST agree with the rest of scripture. Sadly, most 'interpretations' on prayer meetings are wrong, based on personal emotions and poor exegesis. (See my articles on proper interpretation).

Yes, in scripture, people met for impromptu prayers for very serious, urgent reasons (e.g. Peter put into prison). This was when the church at that time met for prayer urgently, <u>every</u> person having been prompted by the <u>Holy Spirit</u> to do so, and not by social pressure or poor teaching. I have never found this one-truth in any prayer meeting that has been scheduled. There is always the pretence of charismatic nonsense of course, but no true believer should copy such demonic influences.

I ask readers to look at what Christ said about praying alone in your room. There is no justification in rejecting or avoiding this matter! Indeed, to carry on regardless of what Christ said is a grave sin.

The Wheat Crunchie Moment

I had a recent fad for eating a cornmeal snack, Wheat Crunchies. After a few months, I 'went off' eating them and stopped, after finding the taste had outrun its tastiness. (Too much of a good thing?).

I attended many prayer meetings and finally had to admit they did nothing for me, and I did nothing for them. I found nothing of God in them and stopped attending. It was my Wheat Crunchie moment! Much later I researched my anecdotal dislike and discovered that my distaste was biblically correct. For me, to continue attending prayer meetings was like eating foods I no longer liked or needed. Of course, liking a command of God is irrelevant to its authority and my duty or love to comply. Which is why I had to finally write articles and then a book, to show that corporate prayer meetings on a schedule are not of God, but of man's meddling.

It is a fact that almost everything done in a traditionalist church is by order of men. That is why we, as a church, examined every little jot and tittle to see if what we said, believed or did in the past, was of God. Sadly, most of it wasn't. So, we started all over again until we obtained valid and genuine scriptural truth. Prayer meetings per schedule had to go! We had no option.

My book explains the entire reason for not holding standard prayer meetings, and my findings, shared with the church and discussed in depth, became our test of obedience. As with every other aspect of church life, we studied for a long time before re-adopting anything of our past, and much of it was rejected. The fact is there in black and white – Christ says we must pray alone in our rooms. Only on rare and specific occasions may we pray with others. And scheduled prayer meetings are not one of those rare occasions!

When the Toronto Blessing (see series of books on this) was foisted onto the whole world, I watched hour after hour of charismatic tomfoolery, though some of it was sickening. One video of a huge meeting of 'Christians' had two famed charismatic preachers/leaders. One began to 'speak in tongues' on the stage. The second man stood on the other end of the stage and responded with his own 'tongues'.

They both bantered with each other for about half an hour, throwing out bizarre and stupid 'tongues' pretending they were real. It was dramatic and meant to be entertaining, as both laughed heartily at points, and made out they were talking with each other in an 'angelic tongue'. The crowd in the audience (they were not a congregation) was roaring in approval, clapped, and shouted!

Friends, there is no such thing as charismatic 'tongues' (see my articles on this). They are demonic manifestations, as was all of the Toronto Blessing garbage. Remember how a well-known pastor renounced his 'tongues' after reading my evidences (that is, evidences in scripture)?

Salvation is between me and God. Prayer is the same. Many prayer contents have no business being told to everyone in a room. For the life of me I do not understand why Christians feel compelled to utter supposed prayers every week in front of others! It is just a bad habit. Or, a Wheat Crunchie fad. Search scripture for yourself and find the truth.

The 'round robin' method of making everyone in the room pray, whether or not they wish to, or are prompted to, is horrible. The sudden request for someone to pray is also horrendous. I pray when God prompts me to do so, any time and anywhere. And usually this is silent.

When prayer is silent when amongst others, it corresponds 'in kind' to Christ's demand that we pray alone in our room. We are NOT called upon to expose our deepest feelings and requests to the whole world. Check this out for yourself. It is a straightforward fact! Why have your soul and spirit jaded because of superstitious nonsense? Comply with God, not with traditionalistic, superstitious, man-made demands.

Aha, What About Married Couples?

During one of our Sunday meetings someone said that praying as a couple or even a family is okay because the couple are 'one' in God's eyes. (See my article on being 'one' as a married couple).

My immediate response was 'Hm. Maybe he has a point'. But, when I thought about it, I was compelled to write an article on it. Whilst a married couple are 'one' in God's eyes, in just about all matters, they CANNOT be 'one' in prayer. Why? Because each of us is saved as an individual, and each of us has individual responsibilities before God. Though 'one' in marriage we are not 'one' when it comes to our standing before the Lord. This is because our sins are all individual, and so our repentances are also individual. A husband cannot repent for his wife, or vice versa.

The same argument is then applied to whole families praying together. But, the same objections arise as with scheduled prayer meetings.

There is a caveat, that if both spouses have exactly the same call from God, about the same issue at the same time, then they fulfil the only examples of corporate prayer found in scripture. But, standard everyday prayers should be alone in our closets. Is Christ right in His command, or not? The book on 'Prayer Meetings' contains far more details.

The ONLY Examples

In almost every local church a pastor or speaker gives an opening prayer, then a longer prayer before speaking, and finally a prayer at the end. Are these acceptable?

Yes, because they are representative prayers. They are usually given by pastors or Bible teachers or some other preacher who is in the pulpit at the time. The prayers are general commendations of the church to God, a commendation for God to make the sermon his own, and a final one commending the people to God. Patriarchs uttered similar prayers. Moses did. Jesus did, as did the Apostles. But, in each and every case, they only prayed because the Holy Spirit prompted them.

Such prayers are not rambling, nor are they mini-sermons! Nor should any speaker utter them unless called by the Spirit to do so. They should be short and to the point, even if they are acceptable. This then obviates human invention and repetition. It is not really corporate prayer, but prayer given by one who speaks pastorally on behalf of everyone else, commending them to God. Such prayers should not stray from that purpose.

Chapter 7

Betters and Minions

'Betters' are those individuals held in highest regard in society. 'Minions' are underlings who serve under a more powerful person, and their work is considered to be servile or unimportant. On a national or international scale, some pastors or speakers are held up high as samples of excellence. They might be – but does God allow us to so vaunt fellow humans, when anything good they say or do is from God anyway?

Traditionalism treats a pastor as the 'better', and everyone else as minions. We see this in the usual traditionalist hierarchy in almost all churches. Even the most enlightened churches treat 'the pastor' with not just respect but with a servile attitude. Whether or not he is worthy of this adulation is not considered. We must just obey and adulate him. Full stop, whether he is good or bad, filled with holy knowledge and understanding, or not. It is his rightful status and our duty to do so. So they say, and so such churches fail badly.

I hear many complaints, if not rage, at this! Even so, it is a truism. The pulpits in churches are not there just so as the congregation can hear and see the speaker. Pulpits are also visual reminders that a pastor/preacher is above everyone else. And 'looking up' at a pulpit proves it.

It is an observable fact in so many churches worldwide, that an hierarchy exists. Starting from the top this is:

1. Pastor (Usually only one)
2. Assistant pastor (if there is one)
3. Elders (even though a pastor IS an elder)
4. Deacons (who think they can choose eldership as a 'promotion')
5. The congregation (which also include minions such as Sunday School teachers, caretakers, and so on).

Is this hierarchy an actual entity, or am I making it up? Of course it is real, even when it is modified to appear to be more liberal.

In scripture there is no hierarchy. Every Christian is an equal member (though those awful groups called 'cliques' do not show it), and those with more public roles given by God, including pastors etc., are equal to each other, though in many places this 'equality' is only superficial... the hierarchy continues throughout history, and those 'at the top' insist on maintaining it, regardless of scripture.

I still remember the sombre way deacons were elected. Each member write down who they thought should be a deacon. The name with the most votes, wins. So, someone who 'puts himself about' wins more votes, and friends and families stick together, so THEY get voted for, too. Does anyone vote for a man who is humble and does not like the limelight, and who possesses all the attributes given in scripture for such a role?

Deacons think their roles are part of the higher hierarchy and will even ingratiate themselves to members in order to get more votes. To be a deacon is a status symbol! But, not in scripture. Oh how a little pride and power goes a long way!

Deacons are simply men (and women, as scripture proves) who can do practical things in the churches, such as laying tables ready for meals, cleaning up, visiting the sick, maintaining any monies, and so on. Thus, a deacon is a functionary of the local church. He is not higher than anyone else, nor is he lower. A deacon with a penchant for a particular task (e.g. carpentry) is recognised by God as suitable, and the man or woman is then called upon to perform those tasks he is good at (by God's decree). This goes for every role within a local church.

A deacon deals with mundane but necessary tasks within a local church… mundane to him but praised by the Lord. No deacon needs to be 'elected' – his skills will be obvious, and so he is automatically a deacon. And there is no reason to replace him/her regularly unless a deacon falls ill or dies or moves away. There is no 'officer' status.

The deacons are just ordinary members who perform certain non-spiritual tasks well. He or she exists to free-up a pastor or Bible teacher for spiritual tasks. In the New Testament even apostles are called deacons, because of their servanthood!

What of elders? Many bigger churches have a number of people they refer to as 'elders', but their status and tasks are often very confused. A 'pastor' is an 'elder', and an 'elder' is just a 'presbyter', and a 'presbyter' is just a 'bishop'. All names for the same person! None of the names is a title of officer status. There is an 'office', meaning a position to fill, but such offices are not status symbols. Everyone, pastor, deacon or the cleaner, are all equal. No one member is greater, or more lowly, than anyone else.

Every Christian has a ministry to perform, though you would not think it when looking at a congregation. They duly arrive on a Sunday or some other day, and sit fairly quietly chatting to each other in their favourite pews. Some unwrap their sweets in readiness, so as to avoid detection by the 'silence police'. 'The' pastor is in a back room with his elders and deacons, chatting or sometimes praying. They come out to the main church at a defined moment and the congregation suddenly become quiet. It might look like respect, but it is merely tradition.

And so the usual 'service' begins with the usual format (see book on Prayer Meetings) and the usual silence of the congregation. This 'order of service' is often referred to as the 'sandwich'.

The man in the pulpit speaks non-stop for about an hour, and his usual prayer can itself take a long time. Any longer and members start looking at their watches! Hymns are sung… but, how many singers know what the hymns mean, and how many sing automatically, not realising the words they use? And how many remember the hymns even a few hours later? The 'service' ends, the speaker/pastor goes to the front door and shakes hands with everyone who leaves. Smiles all around until the next 'service'.

There are no questions in this kind of sandwich, which runs like clockwork as a preconceived whole containing various fillings controlled by the hierarchy.

It is why members may fall asleep, or hold up their eyelids with matchsticks! It is why no-one really learns anything and no-one asks questions. It is simply what we do on a Sunday. No wonder younger folks are bored!

Communion
Communion 'services' used to amuse me when I was a member of this hierarchical structure in traditionalist churches.

Usually, communion is dealt with after a normal service. The large table up front is covered with a linen cloth, and the communion bits and pieces are placed on top, often themselves covered with a napkin. Around the table, usually on a raised platform, sit the deacons (and so-called 'elders' if they have them). The pastor sits centrally facing the congregation. All this is a visual reminder of the illicit hierarchy and the top-dog position of the pastor. Meanwhile the congregation are hushed.

In itself this silence is farcical. Look at the first communion instituted by the Lord Christ; it was brought about 'naturally' as the apostles sat around the low table on cushions. They were chatting to each other and enjoying each other's company, while they had food and drink. Of course, they respectfully shut up when Christ spoke (because He earned such respect always), but otherwise they acted normally. Christ gave His new ordinance and they all partook. The only reason Christ was the 'head' of this activity, is that it was the first time and He had to explain what He was doing. Today it does not matter who hands out the bread and wine.

The point being that communion was part of a meal, and everything was normal. Is the hush in a modern communion really about reverence for Christ's sacrifice? No, not really. Perhaps on a few occasions it is. I offer as evidence the fact that everyone usually chats loudly with each other before the pastor comes in. They tell jokes and talk about their day, or their jobs, or their shopping. The pastor and cohorts enter and there is an immediate silence! Suddenly, their general chatter becomes reverence. Really?

The pastor stands and prays. Maybe elders or deacons do the same. Everything is artificially sombre as deacons bring around the elements of bread then wine. The session may end with a prayer. Then, the chattering begins again! So sombre.

You might think I am arguing against the chatting. No, I am talking about being artificially sombre because it is expected, not because everyone is paying reverence to the activity or to Christ. It is separated from a light meal, which was central to communions in the early churches. And how many have something against a fellow member? They still take the communion and do not heed the warning to put things right before taking communion.

Real communion, then, is part of a light meal (scripture tells us that it was light, and not a substitute for eating a full meal at home). At a meal people sit around and eat, drink and chat. When the communion part comes about there is a natural sombriety, but it is not faked or made unduly sombre by convention! Communion is a time to remember the sacrifice of Christ, and this deserves a sobre mind and heart, but not a pretence of sobriety or reverence. Communion does not need an hour of prayers and speeches. It needs a reminder of why communion is taken, during a socially-spiritually pleasing moment together.

There is no rule in communion about how many times it should be undertaken. However, I urge folks not to make it scheduled regularly, because anything that is scheduled becomes unduly fixated and solidified, with no extemporaneousness. In other words, it becomes just a habit with no true meaning. Only a few words of remembrance are needed. See how Christ Himself did not preach a sermon or pray long prayers. It was probably over with in just five minutes.

Today, communion should be shared, not administered by a team of 'betters'. There is no need for deacons or a pastor to pass out the bread and wine. Nor is it necessary for a pastor to 'lead', to pray, or to deliver another sermon. Anyone can pass around the two elements, because everyone partakes equally. I hope you now have a better idea of what communion is and how it is done. Don't become set in concrete by traditionalism!

Traditionalism pushes 'ordinary' members right down the scale. Throughout this book I am trying to show readers that each one of them is of value to the Lord and 'has a say'. But, in traditionalist churches this is not so. Anyone not in the higher hierarchy must shut up and listen. Think not? It all depends on who you are...

I have described this incident before: the church suddenly found out it had rampant woodworm, making some parts of the building unsafe. An urgent call went out for gifts to cover the costs. No-one (including myself) bothered to ask if the building had just run out of its usefulness. Or, if a building warranted such a huge expense.

Anyway, at that time I was working as an odd-job man at a time of unemployment. I only had what I earned in any week. But, one week I gave my entire earnings to the assistant pastor, and it went into the coffers. I honestly thought I should do so.

The following Sunday, the pastor named another contributor, who happened to be one of the 'leading' members, for her magnificent contribution… which happened to be less than my whole-week earnings. She was praised for being so generous (from a large income that wouldn't miss it). My name was not mentioned.

My point is NOT that my name was missing, but that a richer person of influence in the church, gave a smaller amount and yet received high praise. It instantly showed me I was merely a nameless minion of no importance. I wasn't looking for praise or even for my name to be mentioned. But, the way it was done made me feel insignificant in that church; one of the 'great unwashed'. Can you see what I am getting at?

In another church I attended a few years before, a far more serious incident took place. It was usual for the pastor to take an afternoon session of questions and answers. A good idea. Questions were written down and handed to him for the following week. No problem with that.

One Sunday he answered one of my own questions. Then, I made a fatal mistake that altered his attitude towards me. His answers were anecdotal (again, nothing wrong with that), so all I did was ask "Yes, thanks, but what does scripture say?"

The man next to me was a friend of the pastor and was himself pastor of another church. I heard him draw in his breath slowly, I looked at him and he said "Uh-oh – now you've done it! You've made an enemy." The pastor at the front had a look of ice on his face and he grimly said he would answer another day. But, he never did, and from that moment on I was definitely out of favour and was treated as a nobody, a minion of no value and deserving of no answers.

So, friends, there are definite hierarchical 'rulers' in most of our churches, and there are definite minions, whose ideas and persons are of no value, unless they support the hierarchy. Think about it – can you really see the true structure in your local church? Or, have you been downplayed for so long, you think it is normal and of God?

Chapter 8

Baptism

For small local churches this can be a problem, especially if those churches meet in houses. So, how should we deal with baptism?

Often, members were baptised in other churches before becoming members of a small gathering. But, if not, and someone wishes to comply with God's demands, what happens?

There are no hard and fast rules. In our church I have baptised three or four in a swimming pool in Croatia, when on holiday. My brother-in-law baptised someone in the sea recently (because there is no biblical rule to say only a pastor must baptise).

Now, baptism is a requirement, because it shows everyone that you have been saved, and are now proving your loyalty and praise for the Lord by openly taking part in His instructions. Baptism itself does not save; it is a symbol of your commitment and real faith. Also, baptism MUST be whole-immersion and not partial or sprinkling. (See articles on baptism). This, however, can present with a problem.

It is not always feasible to use a beach or a swimming pool, so what then? Some have managed to hire a local church's baptistry, perhaps on a day when that church is not holding meetings. Other than the above, one might have to become creative.

The main aim is to baptise. This means to fully immerse the person's body under water. This is because, as scripture tells us, baptism is an image of laying down in the grave and then being resurrected. Therefore, whatever means are used will need to make sure the body being baptised is under the water for a brief moment: in-out!

The creative bit is the real challenge. If none of the above are available, why not buy a large children's paddling pool? Then, instead of standing up, the one who baptises (who may, or may not, be a pastor) kneels along with the candidate, who may sit down (kneeling by the candidate can cause a problem). A few words are/or are not spoken and the candidate is gently taken backwards and immersed fully, before being immediately helped back up again.

Another possibility is if someone has a large enough bath or similar equipment… the candidate lays in the water and the one baptising merely tips him or her back so the head is covered. Perhaps there may be other creative ways. So long as the body is fully immersed there is no real problem. Even a pool which is part of a river might be used (though cold).

Where nothing is available we need to be patient. The Lord knows the heart and knows the circumstances! If the local church is willing and a candidate is truly wishing to comply, God will somehow provide an answer.

As for an 'order of service'... look at how Jesus was baptised. He simply walked into the water and John baptised him by full immersion. It took just a few minutes and very little was said. It is not up to a pastor to make everything look more spectacular or theatrical.

What if someone is ill or has a condition meaning he or she is unable to get out of bed or comply otherwise? It is not my task to force anyone to be baptised, or to make someone who is unable to move to comply in the usual way, by ruthlessly making them do so, or otherwise feel a failure or somehow ungodly. Two things apply – the desire of the candidate to comply, and the proper following of God's command. Just as we might have to wait until we can find a suitable way of doing a baptism, so we might have to think of other means when it comes to someone who is unable by reason of illness or condition. It could be that the person might never be able to be baptised. The Lord knows that person's heart and how baptism might on times be impossible. In no way is he or she less than acceptable by God or by the congregation.

God knows the heart of every soul on earth. He knows when there is a true desire to be baptised. And He knows when such seems impossible. And maybe it will remain impossible. We are not enforcers who make sure someone is baptised or else! I can assure readers that there are times when we are faced with such serious conundrums.

If unable at the time to think of ways to bring about such a baptism, we must wait on the Lord. That is all I can say. It might be possible to, say, baptise someone who is wheelchair bound. But, bed-bound is another thing altogether. And if someone is seriously ill and wants to be baptised, we are not free to kill them off by insisting on putting them into a cold-water container!

With the candidate's insistence even a bed-bound individual can be baptised. Here are practical warnings – if anything adverse occurred because such a baptism is done, there could even be legal ramifications. Is it not better to let God do the thinking in these cases? Stay creative and be open to other ideas. The candidate is willing but his or her body may not be able. God knows the heart, so we should not force decisions.

The real scenario is that a person wants to be baptised, and has previously shown their saved status. The baptism is certainly part of our witness, but if such is impossible in our eyes, then that person is STILL accepted by the Lord and is righteous.

As you can see, saying we must be baptised is one thing, but there are times when this normal activity has problems to overcome. If they can be overcome.

Remember that even if it is impossible to baptise someone, that person is still saved by grace by faith alone. His or her desire is to comply and perhaps in some cases it is this inner desire that provides an answer. No pastorate is in black and white! Yes, many texts give us absolute guidelines, but not always. So, we need to think hard and prayerfully wait for answers.

Should a person be re-baptised, if, say, their beliefs have changed? For example, what if the candidate was once a Roman Catholic and was baptised by a priest. Well, Romanist baptism is not true baptism, so a future baptism in truth is needed.

Now, the former Catholic will know in his or her heart that a true baptism needs to be done. He might have been genuinely saved many years before and is now living a true Christian life. Once he or she is advised, it is their responsibility to come forward for baptism. No fellow Christian should nag them or make ultimatums. Also, if that person has a condition that might prevent baptism, baptism might not be physically possible. Though all believers might accept that baptism is required, each is saved by grace as an individual, and the individual's will and spirit must lead the way.

Baptism is one of only two ordinances given by God that we should obey. Communion is the other. There are no other ordinances. Some try to say that baptism saves. But, it does not! It is a public sign that someone has been <u>already</u> saved, and now wishes to testify openly that this has occurred.

Romanists and others have twisted the ordinance, to make it seems salvic. It is NOT salvic at all, but a recognition that salvation has already taken place.

Otherwise, an insistence that baptism saves goes against God's truth. He tells us that we are elect in eternity and that because of this eternal will of God, a person WILL be saved at some time in his/her lifetime. Now, this applies to actual salvation, not to later baptism. This is because any baptism is a PART of salvation and is not a second action needed to save someone.

As with all aspects of doctrine, be careful, define only as scripture defines, and add no personal agenda.

Chapter 9

It is No Romance!

Pastorship and church membership are not romantic esoteric occupations! Yet, so many young men enter into a pastorate thinking they will somehow gain status and an odd form of fame. And members of churches have similar ideas, some thinking 'church' is a weird 'romance'… an idea that only feeds on staying locked behind church doors so reality does not creep in.

Few real churches float through church life without flaw or problems. I can guarantee that! As I have shown, I was called to a particular ministry (BTM) about 20 years after being called to teach and pastor informally. The 'formal' call to pastor came about the same time as the outside ministry came about; roughly 36 years ago (to date). And both calls were amidst explosive situations. No romance! Just plenty of mind-boggling, frightening reality.

There is a mind-picture of a pastor, perhaps dressed in a suit and tie (not obligatory!), or smart casuals, sitting in his study, with shelves full of theology books, and maybe a small computer on the desk. If you visit for an intimate chat or advice, he sits calmly with his legs crossed, and hands in a sort-of 'holy' position, as he listens quietly. If he is a product of a Bible school, he will usually just wait for you to do all the talking. In this way he tries to gather together clues about your situation, so he can make some kind of answer. *(Some are taught to look 'inadvertently' at a fellow's library. What a mistake in my case! I have given many books away because I can get information on computer, but in my remaining library are books that will perplex – all reference books and covering a very wide range of material, including textbooks of heresies or cults).*

But, mainly, he will say as little as possible; again because of college training. And any answers he might give are often products of the same college training, rather than straightforward co-speaking with the one who is troubled. In this way he thinks of his college 'patter' as suitable for all situations.

In many cases like this, the pastor tries to apply his 'training' rather than listen with open spiritual ears and giving a proper biblical answer. As I have said before, there is no 'one size fits all'!!

Yes, there are admirable exceptions to this almost robotic activity, but very few. I have heard and seen too much, and I have listened to the 'playback' from Christians. Once again, you can see my objections are NOT to good men who attend Bible colleges, but to good men who are not called by God to the pastorate or teaching, and are instead going after their personal wishes and peculiar reasons. Such men, though genuine, are not called and this is why so many 'burn out' after a few years.

All you need do to find out that pastorates and churches are NOT romantic, is to take a look into the private world of both, removing those rose-tinted glasses. It is an odd truism that most who attend local churches, even good ones, have no idea about the reality of church life. This is because they are cloaked in the false comfort of traditionalism, which over the last two centuries, has given attendees a false sense of security... so long as they don't go outside their four walls and taste the coffee, and they ignore the open spiritual warfare that is raging around them.

Please understand, I am not just exercising my right to be nasty! I am trying to be as open and honest as possible. I spent so many decades under traditionalism that I am now thoroughly allergic to it! Of course, readers are free to dismiss what I say, which would be very sad. The fact is, we must realise what is truth before we can change to what is better. If we don't find it, we will just muddle along, being of no real use to man nor beast – or God.

I can assure you that pastoring, when done with open heart and biblical mind, is hard work at times. It can be VERY hard... again, nothing romantic at all, and nothing like college training. Tough situations will come along, needing your input and help. So, your life becomes frustrating and sometimes plunged into deep pools of bad things. You should be with me when I cannot sleep for nights on end, because of a bad situation, or Christians who refuse to obey God or repent. This is in addition to my own personal problems or needs.

In my distant past when I was a professional artist (60s and 70s), I immersed myself in my work. I thought I was on my way to possibly worldwide fame as an artist, and things appeared to move that way, such was my activity at that time. Inevitably, I came across art critics, whether of my work or someone else's. Frequently, I had to laugh, sometimes in derision, at critics who had the temerity to tell everyone what this or that artist 'meant' by his various artworks. They tried that on myself and I usually answered with "Well, I painted it because I wanted to – loved the shapes, colours, etc". Their attempt at being ever-so intellectual failed miserably!

Likewise, in pastorship, many think they can apply college-trained answers to spiritual queries and to normal church life. Yes, they CAN do this – but to no avail. The called-pastor has to think on his feet, and must always hand over matters to the Holy Spirit. When God moves us He does so individually, even if several in that church do the same things, or if some situations appear to be similar. It would be a fatal error to treat the whole church as one for intellectual purposes. We each stand ALONE before God in the matters of salvation, repentance, and obedience. If everyone understood this and moved with the same attitude and understanding, then, and only then, can we say the local church acts together with one accord.

Then, we come to ministries

My research work started in 1973 when I began training as a psychiatric nurse. Almost immediately, I could see glaring problems with psychiatry and started to document my responses. Some of my responses agreed with what I was taught, but most did not and I began to work parallel to my training, heeding my beliefs rather than fake psychiatric 'treatments'. So, I started to formulate my own hypotheses. By 1980 I finally completed an initial manuscript that looked at Christians and 'mental illness'. The only reason it was not published is based on a very odd experience: a journalist was interested in my work and asked to borrow the whole manuscript (in three manuscripts) to examine and write up about. Being naïve I gave it to her and said I would collect it again in a month.

Oh dear! I returned to her home to collect the manuscripts. She handed them to me with an apology, claiming she 'lost' the third manuscript containing ALL the references in the book! I was stunned. How on earth could she 'lose' it?? I had no option but to return home without the references. Without these I was unable to publish. This was because it was typed, and I had no copies.

But, the book required several years of intense research, and many contacts with clinics around the world, some of which I was invited to see for myself. The contacts, though, were all in the reference section. So, that was the end of that, though I was able to used parts of the manuscript to write my MA thesis. This was later inserted into a later book.

This background in research continues to today, whether in the pastorate or in my 'parachurch' ministry of BTM. Both ministries, as far as I am concerned, are linked, as one affects the other. And both use research to come to solid conclusions. It is fair to say that every topic I tackle is (a) prompted by God, and (b) properly researched. A pastor who does not do this 'due diligence' is bound to fail, both spiritually and intellectually.

You might say "But, I have not been educated above school level". My friends, this has nothing to do with how high-flying you are, or not. It is about being called by God to pastor or teach. This is not about gaining certificates. As I have said elsewhere, a lot of motive behind my own background was a feeling of inadequacy. It drove me to start with certificates, then diplomas and then degrees. Some from Bible schools and some not. When I first started teaching I did so with just an art school certificate and a nursing qualification behind me!

It took until I was in my late thirties to get as far as an HND, which quickly led to a teaching Diploma and then a BEd (I was invited to finish with another year for Honours, but ran out of grant). Though I finished with distinctions, I still felt inadequate, thinking maybe they had made a mistake! I felt driven to do more, so went through two bachelors, one Masters and then the PhD. I had to prove to myself that I could do it; it is a great motivator! Perhaps, looking back, it was pathetic, but at the time it was a very real inner drive. On the other hand, maybe it was God's way to push me out of my shell, to do His business.

But, my point is that when I began in ministry it was low-key and I was not Bible school 'trained'. However, the Lord made sure I gained knowledge fast and constantly, so I knew as much as any Bible-school trained pastor or teacher. This is what God does for EVERY man He has chosen to these ministries. So, if you are not 'trained' DO NOT feel inferior to Bible-trained men. If you have been called and commit your tasks with utmost sincerity and willingness to learn, then you are a pastor or teacher. And if you don't know something, just ask someone who does. Today, I am still 'low key' not wishing to draw attention to myself for its own sake.

However, the Lord has drawn me into a variety of high-profile tasks, ones I did not seek or sometimes want. I have already mentioned these, beginning with what appeared at first to be nothing to do with faith and God – AIDS. At the time I was fascinated by the topic even before it hit the headlines. This was because what was being said in TV and radio interviews did not make sense at all, and sounded like very bad research.

Over about three years and worldwide contacts, I produced my findings. This is a story in itself, and will not be recounted here, but it had <u>everything</u> to do with Christians, many of whom believed the government (much as they did with the false pandemic of Covid in the 2020s). it was then that I saw the often imperceptible ties between the world and Christian beliefs and actions.

This was followed by research into Islam and the murderous intentions of jihadist Muslims. Then came the Toronto Blessing and its evil destruction of churches and lives. And so my ministry has gone on from one 'hard' topic to another, with or without my desire to follow it. In a similar way, the Covid deception has been the latest topic I have had to tackle. This time I began by studying it with London University, very soon after I heard about it. But, my belief in the reality of Covid quickly disappeared as God caused me to research in more depth. The result was almost two years (to the time of writing this book) in-depth study of a non-existing 'pandemic' with a 'virus' dressed to look different, but which was and is a weak flu, albeit man-made.

Why write about these topics? Because I am a pastor and must guide those who are my fellow church members, to whom I have a charge from God. A pastor is responsible for guidance at all levels and for all purposes, insofar as he is able. The task is not just about making sure everyone is spiritually safe; it is about everything in life. It does not mean you are qualified in every topic, only that you know where to get information from the right quarters.

This includes your own research, and asking God to lead you to the right sources. So many Christians have been misled and deceived by Covid, and this has led to their deaths and to a refusal to accept Christian answers. Hence the topic is essential, even though huge numbers of believers try to avoid or side-line what I say; instead, they believe anything said by a corrupt government – and most think it is all about a virus, when in reality it is about socialists (Marxists etc) using a weak to make people afraid. Why? So, in true Marxist fashion, they cling to the very ones who made-up the horror, as if they were saviours. It is a terrible indictment of modern Christians who shift from Christ as Saviour to evil men wanting us to submit to communism!

I hope you can see that churches are not just repositories of people who have specific beliefs. They are gatherings of Christians who are, hopefully, like-minded (because they believe the same doctrinal truths) and who care for each other. This is why church members must all be taught in what constitutes truth in any matter. They must also be carefully led to important information when it comes to their physical and emotional wellbeing. More than that, every Christian must be taught how to critically analyse all of life, including the latest news items.

As I have taught many times, of all people, Christians MUST have a well-developed (and used) sense of critical analysis. That is – they must think for themselves and not be duped by church or secular authorities. Of course, we can all be duped at SOME time, but if we have critical faculties firing on every piston, we will all the more quickly discover the facts and put things right. (Or, if this is not possible, to at least know the truth in any situation). Those who sit passively in pews while one man speaks for an hour, without questions or comments, will not hone these skills of mind and heart, so are easy victims of spiritual (and other) fraud.

A Pastor's Own life

Everyone must sharpen their spiritual senses. This particularly applies to pastors who would otherwise be at a disadvantage when it comes to guiding the flock of Jesus Christ. So, while he must expect AND TEACH the need for critical analysis of everything that happens in this world, he must firstly discipline his own mind to be critical of all claims, whether by scholars, theologians, scientists or governments. And also of those members who are his brethren in the local church.

This applies continuously. During the writing of this book, my dear wife died, and I put it aside for a short while. However, apart from one Sunday without taking a meeting, I continued to teach the book of Job every week, which blessed me enormously. Then, when it was completed, I published a longer version (I was adding to the book in tandem with teaching each chapter, so the publication of the book was swift). I later continued to write this book, though the loss of Diane still affects me every day. Pastors must keep going, friends! The world does not stop because of a personal tragedy. However, one must ask – who looks after the pastor? He deals with everyone else's problems, but who cares for the pastor? This is a general, not a personal, question.

As I have said to others, the pastor is a lonely person. He cannot share what God has given to him personally to do. It thus behoves his fellow members to simply observe him in his daily life. Does he need help, or comfort, or counsel?

Having said that, one of the biggest comforts I have had in times of distress (and I have had many), has been my calling to pastor and to continue with my parachurch ministry. Without them I would have been as affected as the next man. It is how God looks after His own. No, I do not mean my calling is just a crutch (as Karl Marx claimed), but it is certainly of immense personal help.

I find my calling all-consuming and it does not stop. I think of it daily and when I go to sleep. I awaken thinking about what I am to do that day. At the moment of writing this, I know that throughout the day I will have 'pop-up' thoughts about my wife, because her command by God to go home is still fresh. And yet my work continues unabated. If anything, now I have no wife, my time spent at ministry is very much extended every single day and into the evening. This is because when God calls us to do something it must be all-out or not at all. HIS work comes first, not our own. Yes, I would sincerely want my wife, but now she has gone I must continue.

We should not be thinking how to fit our lives around our ministry (every Christian has a ministry), because such thinking means we place God's word on par with our own, or with our interests, orf even at a lower level. No, a calling is constant and is undertaken as and when God calls. Thus, He comes first and everything else must make allowance for it, or be put aside, including secular work and times of rest. This is so even if we are ill or tired or 'stretched out'. We must not put off God's work because we say we have no time. Our time on this earth is very limited. We don't know if our time will end in the next hour, week, or year. So, we must just get on with it whilst we have the time and strength. Having a calling from God is full-time, if only in our thinking.

Whilst writing this portion I received emails from someone in Sweden, who wrongly said she had BPD (Borderline Personality Disorder: See my articles on this topic) and was unable to change, though she is a Christian. I sent her two emails giving the facts, and saying that what she had was not an illness but a behavioural sin. I received an email back thanking me for my 'advice' and saying that from now she would call on God to be more involved in her 'illness'.

She is NOT ILL, but she chose to misinterpret what I said, to suit her desire to remain 'ill' (and therefore not responsible for all her gross sins, from violence, to suicide attempts, to wrong ideas about God, etc). Time and time again people show that they prefer to be 'ill' than to do what God says. It is a way of avoiding responsibility, even for Christians.

This kind of deliberate tinkering with true counsel and biblical facts is rife. Even those you know might come out with similar misinterpretations so they can continue in their sins. It is why face-to-face discussions are essential when dealing with sin and wrong motives. You might argue that you know nothing about BPD or psychiatric complaints. You are probably correct in that assumption – BUT, it is not about psychiatry, it is about SIN. So, if you are a genuine pastor called to your role by God, and a fellow member shows such problems, you ARE qualified to speak and help. However, such help can sometimes have to be handed-over to secular 'experts'. Not because they are right or good for the 'sufferer' but because the 'sufferer' refuses godly counsel.

Today, psychiatry is taken to be a medical branch. But, it isn't. It is just a patchwork of 'educated guesses'. Sometimes it says something useful, but mostly it imparts eastern mysticism, atheism, and many godless theories. Which brings us to pastors advising members to go see a doctor for 'mental' problems…

Just because a person's presenting 'symptoms' are gross or mind-blowing and complex, does not mean the pastor without knowledge should pass the person on to psychiatry (unless there is a need to, sometimes because of potential legal problems)!

From many years observation and experience, I must say that psychiatry is a paper-tiger. It is based mainly on unbelieving texts and studies, written by unbelieving 'experts'. But, their problem is that they miss out the spiritual realm. This is inevitable because they are unsaved and have no idea what they are talking about. (See my book on psycho-babble).

Put it this way – most people who seek counsel for their 'mental' problems do not have mental problems at all. Their problems are down to emotional dysfunction. Their mental state is unfortunately blasted into submission by their poor emotional functions. And these are misguided by their bad spiritual functions! To a pastor who has no idea at all about psychiatry, all this is beyond their realm, so they pass people on to unbelieving 'experts'. Big mistake! Especially if you are dealing with Christians.(Note: I do not offer counsel to unbelievers, because without being saved they cannot respond to God or His laws).

One Christian man I counselled (after he requested a meeting) spoke to me of his problems. I identified certain factors and advised him his 'symptoms' were those of spiritual malfunction. I also gave him steps to take to be rid of them. He accepted, but then soon afterwards entered a mental hospital, despite my warning never to do so. After a few weeks he discharged himself and admitted that everything I had said was true and my warning about a hospital was justified. After that he lost his 'symptoms'.

Pastors invariably come across Christians with 'mental' problems. In my experience, if there are no hidden causes discovered by 'differential diagnosis' (examinations to see if there is physical causation), then the various 'symptoms' are caused NOT by anything physical or 'mental', but by a poor spiritual attitude and function. To put it in ordinary words, when a person refuses to hand-over his whole life to God, and does not act in true spiritual manner, he will fall down, often badly. Mostly, his malfunction is due to having emotional problems, which are, in turn, affected by poor spiritual function. This should be well within the remit of any pastor.

However, such 'symptoms' can become so bad that the pastor has no choice but to hand the person over to doctors. To do so is NOT failure, but right thinking. This is because they are serious malfunctions showing the refusal of the person to give their lives to God, but a wish to live sinfully. So, someone who attempts suicide, develops eating disorders, and so on, have proved they have moved outside God's word, and so a pastor may be ineffective, simply because the 'sufferer' is not listening to godly counsel and wishes to remain in their sin. When this happens a pastor has no option but to pass the person on to a secular authority, for legal and personal reasons, even if the person claims to be saved. (See my book on disobeying God's laws). The reason is simple – the erring person will otherwise drain the pastor of his strength and thinking, so he becomes a victim of sin just as much as the badly erring 'Christian'.

It is possible that a person with such bad symptoms, is being affected by demonic influence, but when those symptoms risk life, he or she must be given over to secular authorities, to avoid a legal problem. I cannot give advice on demonic influence in this book, because it is not something I can cover in just a few words. Demonic influence is NOT demonic possession – no believer can be possessed, but he CAN be heavily influenced, if he has somehow lost his way as a Christian and allows evil to penetrate his mind. If he wore the 'whole armour of God' it would not happen, though Satan will certainly try. (See separate articles on this topic). In the past I have dealt with possession and influence.

So, a pastor who is faced with these demonic actions should, if necessary, seek counsel from other believers who are familiar with them and how to negate their activities. At any rate, the pastor should never be afraid of such forces, but must command them to go in Jesus' Name. At no time should a pastor encourage individual Christians to follow counselling courses, which are usually founded on rewritten secular theories. And, even when a totally

Christian source of information is used (e.g. Jay Adams, etc), it is made useless because the 'counsellor' is relying on human suggestions rather than on God alone. And, he must have the cooperation of the 'suffering' Christian.

As you can see from the above, there is nothing remotely 'romantic' about being a pastor! Unless being slapped in the face and enduring long periods of tough decisions and even tougher circumstances are somehow 'romantic'! However, individual members can also have big problems. It is their role to try to negate bad events and conditions, rather than simply hand everything over to a pastor!

You can also see why so many pastors are burnt-out and leave their positions. This is what happens when a man is not called by God to be a pastor, but sees it as a profession or a job, or, that is how the local church sees it – they pay a salary (stipend) so they want their pound of flesh! It also happens because churches pay for a pastor and then pile tons of duties on his shoulders, often unrealistically. I have already said that even one 'sermon' a week can be tough-going. So, to add many other duties on top is unthinking and unrealistic, if not unbiblical.

Sadly, though, a huge number of men think that simply by attending a Bible college, and ending up with their diploma/degree, that this is their 'qualification' to pastor! Not so. Because of such a false belief, most churches are empty or struggling with boredom and poor teaching. The ONLY qualification needed is to be called by God. When a man is truly called by God, God will give him all the gifts and necessary skills he will ever need. The Holy Spirit will guide his path, and any decisions he has to make. He does not need ultra-knowledge of theology or cults, etc. All he needs is a heart open to God's prompting throughout life.

The proof is in the pudding – his labours will all be in God's Name, and the congregation will see his genuineness. A man who has attended a Bible college might be called to be a pastor, with or without an income. (I have never received an income, nor have many others). I find theological knowledge interesting and useful, but it is not my grounding; my true grounding is God's prompting. What He expects of a pastor is obedience to His word, and openness to the leading of the Holy Spirit, as he guides the flock in holy things. That's it!!

Throughout all this, the congregation is not passive. Every member must work alongside a pastor, or several pastors, and each must perform his or her own ministry. EVERYONE has a ministry! Together, every Christian in a local church can make a huge difference, so long as they ditch every traditionalist notion and only does what <u>God</u> wants of them. A local church that does this is a real family, and it shows before both fellow believers and the unsaved.

Chapter 10

An Overview

Make no mistake about it – most 'ordained' men see independent pastors as lower species. Especially if they hold meetings in their homes. Some think these 'house churches' are inferior, though early Christians met in their homes! Some think a 'house church' is charismatic (which we are not), so look down on their doctrine. I know all this because I come across such misplaced ignorance occasionally.

I was standing on the pavement one sunny day painting my fence, when a member I knew from a local church I once attended walked past. He was on his way to another local church he was not a member of, on the corner of my street. Previously, he admitted he goes there after going to his own church, because they had a good array of tea, coffee and snacks after the services.

He couldn't stop he said, but then, as a parting shot, he said with a smile, "If ever you want to come back to the Church, go to the one I am going to". I stopped myself from replying!

Huge numbers of men who become pastors after attending Bible colleges, have said they did not know what they were going to do after receiving their degree in this or that Bible subject. So, they finally decided on a pastorate to get onto the 'bottom rung', or at least so as to 'get a job'. This is what they have said. The reason they say and do this, is very plain – they have not been called to ANY pastorate or biblical field. And foolish churches pay them stipends (an old name for wages), and usually give them a home rent free, and help with fuel costs, car and travel expenses. Not a bad way to get money, and better than most church members get!

But, the sermons they deliver tend to show their inner disinterest and non-calling. After a while they have itchy feet and want to try for another church with a higher 'status' (and more money). And some who remain become burnt-out because they are controlled by their churches and are overworked.

Another problem is when a pastor is young – such are not found in the Bible, which describes pastors as 'elders' – or 'grey-hairs'... older men, who all appear to arise from within their own local church.

Payment of a wage might apply to pastors who have no other income, but it is a fact that many pastors, even in the 'middle band' get more income in money and 'helps' (heating, electricity, car or car expenses, etc) than the people they pastor. It is not necessary for a pastor to have all these 'perks', which are not listed as such in scripture.

Does this seem sound? Or, fair? I remember with concern how one pastor asked church members to give him a very large loan, so he could move out of the church-provided manse, and into a specially-built large house in its own grounds. The loan was hugely less than a normal mortgage and was repaid quickly.

The house he bought was the size of a country mansion, and was in a quiet village, well away from the pesky congregation. I am sorry to say I viewed the transaction as manipulative and wrong. Everyone else had to pay a mortgage for a home in the city. Think it over. The reason why that pastor wanted a new house was (in his own words) "Because when I retire from this pastorate, I will be left with nothing."

What did he think everyone else had when they retired? His 'reason' was, to my mind, not godly or showing faith. It turned out that soon afterwards, he committed adultery and left that church. But, he had already repaid the loan and so left with his mansion intact. Other pastors 'work their way up' to higher pay and 'better' status, thus enjoying the glory given to them by others and living well, without fear of losing everything, as so many workers do today. In this I see no faith, only raw desires to be 'somebody' and to have a 'career'. Many genuine pastors have no income and yet work tirelessly as servants of the local church, asking for nothing. May the Lord bless them and their efforts.

This kind of fakery is rife amongst the churches. Also, how many pastors are called to be pastors?

Few, it seems, given their traditionalism. Many years ago I was chatting with a fellow member (when we were both in a traditional church) and the topic moved on to who occupies the pulpit. I said that very few appear to be called by God, so they should get out of their pulpits. My fellow believer was horrified, and said "If we did that, there would be hardly anyone to run our churches!" Precisely!

In other words, it is okay to have pastors who have never been called to be pastors, let alone speakers or teachers, so long as someone filled the pulpit! And this kind of belief was uttered by a saved mature Christian!

God always provides His man at the right time in the right place. No need to advertise for a pastorate, or for churches to advertise for pastors. God does it all. But, traditionalist churches do not think this way. And this is why God called me out of the 'system' of traditionalism, so that I could at last be honest and free from the odd beliefs that held me back from being true to the Lord. Yes, those I left behind still think of me as a 'backslider' or 'troublemaker', because it is easier to think that way than to accept that God called me to something better.

This is not a boast, but a fact. In all humility, I can say that my calling by God was, and is, real. I obtained nothing for myself, apart from integrity and God's way of teaching spiritual truths. For these things I am grateful. Those who once pretended to be friends, quickly vanished. Apart from those now in our church, my friends are from outside my home city, both in the UK and abroad. They see God, and not me. Again, I am grateful for this.

I check my motives and work every day. And when I receive hate mail, I do so again, to check that I am really saying what God wishes me to say. Anyone who is called by God will have a similar testimony.

If you are called to be a pastor, you are not called to receive a special title, or money, or status. You are not even called to be a 'leader'. You are called from within your fellow members* to act on behalf of the Chief Shepherd, the Lord Jesus Christ. So, what you do or say is from Him, not yourself. Any glory is for Him, not you. You are, like me, just a servant of the people you meet with in the congregation. (*In God's Church there are no 'official members'. Everyone who is saved is automatically a member of the universal Church, and therefore of any local church they attend. Thus, a 'member' of a local church does not need to be elected by deacons, etc. A 'member' is any saved person who happens to attend a meeting at any time).

As a pastor you will often have very hard work ahead of you, without any kind of recognition. And, at times, especially if you become involved with warring married couples, you may even be blamed for all kinds of mishaps! And if you dare to intervene (BECAUSE you are a pastor and it is demanded of you by God) in marriage disputes, you will not be the couple's 'best friend'! And, anyway, most couples are right on the edge of divorce before they ask you to intervene – IF they ask at all! Even Christian couples can get into this sad, unbiblical position. If you can see potential signs of troubles you must speak, no matter what the couple thinks of your 'interference'. By the time you are involved it may be too late, because couples try to hide their bad condition, and usually decide to part without asking for counsel.

As a pastor you must be "apt to teach". This means you must have Bible knowledge, are able to discern sin from purity, and can apply Bible teachings to a particular person's current state. It does NOT mean, if you are Bible college trained, that you apply academic answers and known counselling techniques to situations. You do not do this because the Holy Spirit is <u>your</u> guide, while you guide the flock. NOT a Bible-college teaching unit, or a well-known preferred counselling guru.

Though trained in psychiatry, I took many years to 'translate' my training into Biblical truth. In effect, it meant I 'rewrote' what I had been taught, so that it was godly and not secular. A Bible college 'training' is in one set of ideas only, following a set-route and preferred theories. It is extra to what scripture says, so the graduate must learn all over again, this time to do what God wishes him to do. Many graduate and never, ever enter a pastorate, or any other 'biblical' activity. In this way, their degree is just like any other degree, and might help to gain paid employment. In my own case, my PhD in theology does not mean I am qualified to be a pastor or Bible teacher. It simply means I have undertaken academic studies for my own sake. Sometimes, God might cause me to hearken back to my various studies, but no study qualifies a man for pastorate or for any other ministry. A call to a ministry is completely separate from academic or any other background. The call from God is THE qualification for ANY ministry. And when a Christian accepts the call he is given gifts and skills necessary. A college does not do this.

Usually, the 'untrained' man knows he has been called, and acts accordingly, regardless of whether or not he is paid for the privilege of being a 'servant to all'. And, usually, because his is a true calling, he will work hard and long at guiding others. Yes, 'trained' men can also be loyal to the Lord and <u>are</u> called... but the predominance of such men being 'traditionalist' is great.

Bible colleges provide much academic material of interest. I can attest to that. But, like all other educational establishments, they rely on – money. And this drives courses and actions along a money-path that is not spiritually healthy, so the money becomes 'filthy lucre'. This is why I am glad that my ministry is not built upon continually pleading for money! I and my co-founder realised early on that money is not the foundation of what we do. The call of God is the foundation and He will give us money, or not, as He wishes. Yes, we do wish we had a larger income (our 'income' for years has been nil, or provided by our own personal money). Now and then the ministry receives gifts, but not enough to pay for much, though we are very grateful for them – every penny counts. However, we know that if we were in the same position as so many other 'ministries' we would be sending out pleas for cash, and that does not rest easily with me. It is why the ministry is low-key; it HAS to be because we have no money, and I am now living on a state pension. The Lord knows all this, and any limits are always in His mind and heart.

And this is how so many independent (of traditionalism) churches survive. Because most meet in houses, there are no extra overheads, and pastors are unpaid. Do not envy pastors who are paid – most are tied to traditionalism and the demands of the members who pay them. Not good!

A pastor (or group of pastors, all co-equal) can help fellow members with all kinds of spiritual teachings. In my own case, for example, I have taught the wickedness of charismatic (and other) heresies, showing why they are heresies and how to combat them. Same goes for the current daily task of keeping Christians informed about Covid 19, so vital because governments are using a supposed virus (no-one has yet properly isolated and identified it) to strip nations of freedom and godly living. It affects Christians very badly and has changed them from being brethren to being enemies, of each other.

In other words, a pastoral role is not limited to Bible texts only. Very often a man can talk fluently in memorised Bible texts (I wish I could!), but there may be no application to the lives of members. We do not live in bubbles. We live in a real and sinful world, and must be ready to combat all kinds of evils. A pastor should help towards this clarity and usefulness.

A pastor, then, has a very important role to play. Yet, he is a servant to all in the local church. He is not the boss, or a political leader, nor is he above others. Scripture says that a pastor who does what he is supposed to do is worthy of double-honour.

> *"Let the elders that rule well be counted worthy of double honour, especially they who labour in the word and doctrine."*
> (1 Timothy 5:17)

This does not mean a pastor must <u>expect</u> double-honour or see it as a kind of social honour. Note what Timothy says – double honour goes to those who labour in the word and doctrine. Just being a pastor does not give such honour.

What is this 'double honour'? It means such a man is to be well thought of and has a spiritual price double that which he is given. Really, it has nothing to do with money or goods. It means that a pastor who is faithful and who teaches true doctrine without fail, is worthy of a show of dignity and to be well-thought-of. If you attend a local church that has such a pastor (or several), you should keep to his company for God sees him as precious. Unlike the very young pastor who told my mother, a godly woman, that she HAD to treat him with honour because he was a 'reverend'! Perhaps you might guess her response to such a show of pride. And mine. (Note: 'Reverend' should not be used by mortal men. It is used only once in scripture, to refer to God Himself. Psalm 111:9).

A man who is called to be a pastor will find himself in a continual round of hard work, whether mentally, physically or spiritually. Fellow members must understand this. Sometimes they forget, and pile work upon work on his shoulders, perhaps inadvertently. He has a heart for every single soul in the church, and this can be exhausting. And his role takes up every single day of the week, including Sundays if he is also the main teacher/preacher. For about 40 years I have only known rest when I physically go away, even if only for a few days. It is important to be physically refreshed.

Do not forget everyone else in the local church. In our own church almost every member does his or her spiritual, mental and physical duty. We all help each other, and others are encouraged continually to participate in whatever gift and role they have been given by God. In this way we act as one, with very few disagreements! It is essential for the pastor to encourage, especially if he is himself older. One day someone else will be called to pastor, so members must be aware of this, and should copy what is good in a pastor, and be ready. The one who then follows should not (as I did at first) try to emulate the late or previous pastor. No, he must simply obey God and guide the flock in good ways, as God demands, as scripture teaches, and in his own way.

Finally. Local churches have their own life and ways. They all do things differently. So long as what they do and say is borne of the Lord, the differences don't matter. Each and every member must learn as much as possible of God's word, and of a Christian way of behaviour. They must learn how to apply God's word to their own lives – every text in scripture has such application, so look for it!

You have been left in no doubt that I think little of traditionalist churches, which often misinterpret scripture. Many of these churches have saved people as members, and sometimes a pastor is led to teach them, whether or not he is Bible-college 'trained'. Such people provide useful biblical teaching (if they are called to do so), but members must watch out for a pastor's heart that is humble and pure. We can all make mistakes, especially when tired or stressed. Pray for your pastor/s. Avoid the stifling effects of tradition. And love each other.

There is far more to say! If you have questions, just ask. But, never assume!

Appendix

Weddings & Funerals

Some denominational priests automatically are enabled to conduct marriages and funerals, e.g. Anglican priests, and are counted to be wedding officiants under the law. This means a priest can marry the couple and then 'make it official' by acting as registrar. But, most independent pastors are not allowed to be registrars.

Weddings can be conducted by pastors of independent churches, but unless they apply to be officiants, such weddings are not legally recognized until the couple later go to a government officiate (e.g. local council Registrar) to 'complete' the process with another ceremony.

This is why I do not conduct weddings, even for our own members, but am happy to give a blessing at a special meeting. It seems that registrars can attend weddings, so long as they are not 'religious'. And applications to become officiates are turned down if the applicant refuses to conduct weddings for people not linked to the local church, or who are homosexuals, etc. Because of these restrictions imposed by government I have not applied to become an officiate. Even if I did, my application would fail, because I would not marry people who are ill-fated or homosexual, etc.

When I considered a wedding at one of the wedding venues now popping up everywhere, in hotels, castles, and so on, I could have conducted the wedding, but the registrar would then have to conduct his or her own ceremony to 'make it legal'. He or she would not actually be in the first ceremony, so timing would need to be good! Because of the complex way this is done, I decided not to conduct the wedding.

Many Christians think they 'must' be married in a church 'before God'. Thus, many seek to marry in a church with a nice-looking entrance, for 'photos. But, in reality, everything we do is 'before God', no matter where we are (so long as the place is not godless or associated with evil activities). You can also marry in one of the many venues advertised as wedding venues, and can be married indoors or outdoors. What matters is the ceremony, which will give the whole thing credibility. Otherwise you will be involved in trying to work out intricate timings and places to satisfy government officials! And if you take advice – whether or not you are an officiate, do not agree to marry a couple you do not know, or if they are unsaved.

As for funerals – any pastor or, for that matter, anyone at all, can conduct a funeral. This is usually done in coordination and association with the funeral director, who is more than familiar with proceedings, and can assist you to prepare a form of service. As with weddings, I advise against conducting a funeral for the unsaved for a number of legitimate reasons.

It is better for the church to understand from the start that you will conduct these ceremonies for members-only, who will be saved anyway. This will help you to avoid outside influences and demands made by unsaved persons. A pastor is for the local saved persons in a church gathering; he is not for unsaved persons and their families.

The wedding conditions imposed by government are unfair, but they should not cause a Christian couple to feel angry or distressed. As the saying goes, "It is what it is", so there is no point in becoming upset. And most wedding parties contain both saved and unsaved persons anyway.

Sadly, most pastors are willing to conduct funerals for unbelievers. This ought not be the case, for their spiritual remit does not cover them for unbelievers, and any eulogy spoken cannot be sincere or spiritually suitable.

Useful Reading From BTM Publications

The full publications' list is attached below, correct up to the end of December, 2021; other titles will have been added following publication of this book. Many titles have been used in our church meetings, or are results of church discussions, and so form the basis for most of this book. They are also for general reading by other Christians. 'Outlines' are very short papers, and 'Articles' are longer with more detail, including Bible texts.

O U T L I N E S

REF.NO.	TITLE
O/01	**Is Man Two-Part or Three-Part?** *(Does a person have body, soul _and_ spirit?)*
O/02	**Bible Versions.** *(Does it matter which version we use? Are they all the same?)*
O/03	**Disfellowship.** *(Casting out of people from the local church)*
O/04	**Temptation.** *(An explanation of what temptation is - it is NOT sin!)*
O/05	**Ecumenism.** *(Is ecumenism Biblical? What about joining with the RCC?)*
O/06	**Denominations.** *(Are denominations valid or are they unbiblical?)*
O/07	**Holy Days?** *(Easter, Christmas and other traditional Holy days... are they Biblical?)*
O/08	**Pastors.** *(Most modern pastors are false, according to scripture itself!)*
O/09	**Roman Catholicism.** *(Why the RCC is a cult and is not Christian)*

O/10   **Creation - Why We Must Believe It.** *(There is no valid alternative to Creation)*

O/11   **Judging Others.** *(Is it okay to judge others? Is it allowed by God?)*

O/12   **What is Doctrine?** *(Is 'love' more important than doctrine? Doctrine is rarely understood)*

O/13   **Church Membership.** *(Is too much made of local church membership?)*

O/14   **Homosexuality.** *(Is it a sin? Or can a 'stable relationship' make it okay?)*

O/15   **Billy Graham - a Man of God?** *(A sober look at this world-known preacher)*

O/16   **Chocolate Soldiers.** *(Are modern Believers cowards - or are we true to God?)*

O/17   **AIDS.** *(A Biblical perspective, plus anecdotal evidence)*

O/18   **Christian Personality.** *(Do we cover up sin by calling it our 'personality'?)*

O/19   **Are Demons Real?** *(Or are they part of imagination or mythical?)*

O/20   **Dangers of Complementary Treatments**

O/21   **Divorce.** *(Can Christians divorce)*

O/22   **The Church of True Israel**

O/23   **Prayer Meetings.** *(A disturbing look at what are called 'prayer' meetings)*

O/24   **The Great Flood & The Ark.** *(Real or just myth? Important? Literal?)*

O/25   **The Devil's Playground.** *(A personal view of mental hospitals)*

O/26   **Ask - Listen - Act!** *(God's blueprint for following Him. Do you do it?)*

O/27   **Quakers - Are They Christian?** *(Or are they members of a cult?)*

O/28   **Worship.** *(What is a 'worship' service supposed to mean?)*

O/29   **Godly Counselling is not Man-Centred.** *(The proper approach)*

O/30   **The 'Love-Them-To-Heaven' Syndrome.** *(A reverse of Godly values)*

O/466   A Sound Mind is Mandatory
O/467   The Congregation of the Dead
O/468   Did Jesus Warn About Hell?
O/469   The UN Drowns-Out Truth About Covid
O/470   Men DO NOT have a 'feminine side'!
O/471   Charismatic Tongues in 1581!
O/472   A Lesson from Job's Wife
O/473   The Nuremberg Code. *(Covid vaccines are illegal)*
O/474   Do Christians Use Circular Reasoning?
O/475   A Note on Miracles
O/476
O/477   Shunning
O/478   Two Types of Levitical Law
O/479   The 'Old Man'
O/480   "This cup…" *Jesus asked for it to be removed*
O/481   Shalom. *NOT a fashion accessory!*
O/482   Generosity? Or Something Else? *What is it?*
O/483   Anglicanism – a Picture of Sin
O/484   Forgive & Forget? It all Depends
O/485   Job – "like a man". *Manliness today*
O/486   John 3:16. *Real interpretation.*
O/487   "My yoke is easy." *Reality for today.*
O/488   Forgive and Forget, 2. *Does God really forget?*

Series on RC teachings

RC/001 The Rock
RC/002 The Popes

OTHER OUTLINES CURRENTLY BEING ADDED

A R T I C L E S

(Any costs shown are the production costs, not prices)

REF.NO.   **TITLE**

A/01   **Are Prayer Meetings Valid?** (Are you honest
        enough to read this one? It is Vital).   *P16…£1.60*
A/02   **What is Christian Freedom?** *(Does it really exist? Do
        some use it to abuse?).**P4…40 p.**
A/03   Nursing & Residential Homes. *(A Christian
        perspective).P18…£1.80 (TO BE REWRITTEN)*

A/04   **Demons Are Real.** *(Demons are real beings, in this world. Be aware).* **P8...80 p.**

A/05   **The Health, Wealth & Prosperity Movement.** *(An evaluation).* **P18...£1.80**

A/06   **Multi-Cultural Schools.** *(What they really mean in the Midlands of the UK).***P6...60 p.**

A/07   **Christians Cannot be Theistic Evolutionists.** *(Evolution in disguise!).***P12...£1.20**

A/08   **Christian Counselling – Fact and Fiction. P6**

A/09   **Transcendental Meditation.** *(An evaluation of this and Yoga).***P6...60 p.**

A/10   **The World Council of Churches.** *(Is the WCC a Christian body?).* **P4...40 p.**

A/11   **Is James 5:14 a Past, Present, or Future Reality?** *(Healing prayer and oil).* **P8...80 p.**

A/12   **Christians and AIDS Care.** *(Error based on misguided emotions).* **P8...80 p.**

A/13   **Evolution Theory in the History of Psychology.** *(Is psychology/psychiatry a 'gift' of God akin to benefits of medicine?).* **P5...50 p.**

A/14   **Is God 'Mother'?** *(Feminism and a theological heresy).* **P4...40 p.**

A/15   **Who Is Reverend?** *(Are pastors free to use the title 'Reverend'?).* **P4...40 p.**

A/16   **The Blasphemy of Gay Christians, so-called.** *(The twisted theology of gays).* **P10...£1**

A/17   **Romans 1 and Homosexuality.** *(What God really says about gays!).* **P12...£1.20**

A/18   **The Great Flood & the Ark.** *(An inspiring account based on Biblical facts).* **P25...£2.50.**

A/19   **Introduction to Christian Personality.** *(Most Christians have a wrong view of personality).* **P10...£1**

A/20   **Behind the Versions.** *(The evil behind certain Bible versions).* **P12...£1.20**

A/21   **'Saved' Children Who are Not. P4/90p**

A/22   **Poverty is Relative.** *(A Biblical look at beggars and Western ideas of poverty).* **P4...40 p.**

A/23   **Fullerism.** (Another Arminian error). *P6...60p*

A/24   **Should We Denounce Others?** A reality-check!

A/25   **Women Priests.** *(Women may not become priests or pastors). **P8...80 p.***

A/26   **Holy Spirit or Hysteria.** *(A serious warning about the Toronto Blessing). **P13...£1.30***

A/27   **Calling Down God's Judgment – Imprecatory Prayer**

A/28   **Did Christ Go Down Into Hell?** *(This common belief is challenged). **P4...40 p.***

A/29   **Easter – or Passover? Acts 12:4.**

A/30   **The Ordaining of Ministers**

A/31A   **"Look Past the Manifestations...". Part One.** *(Important follow-up to A/26). **P13...£1.30***

A/31B   **As above. Part Two.** *P14...£1.40*

A/32   **Tongues** *(Biblical tongues NOT heavenly language, but foreign languages!). **P15...£1.50***

A/33A   **Spiritual Gifts: Part 1** *(misinterpreted and abused by charismatics; undervalued by others!)* **P12...£1.20**

A/33B   **Spiritual Gifts: Part 2.** *P12...£1.20*

A/34   **Charismaticism** *(The true nature of charismatic beliefs and activities). **P14...£1.40.***

A/35   **Fruit of the Spirit.** *(The charismatic claim to 'fruit' is an error. Biblical evidence given).* **P13...£1.30**

A/36   **Assessment of a Toronto Blessing Meeting Led by Rodney Howard Browne.** *P9...90 p.*

A/37   **The Jews Today.** *A biblical truth.*

A/38   **The Jews Today, 2. P16/£2.20**

A/39   **Toronto Help-Line.** *(Explains the need)* **P11...£1.10**

A/40   **The True Spirit of the Toronto Blessing Reveals Itself.** *(Disturbing trends of the TB).* **P7...70 p.**

A/41   **Animal Rights & Pet Culture** *(Biblical?)*

A/42   **Jesus in the Old Testament.**

A/43   **The True Spirit of the Toronto Blessing Revealed, No.2.** *(A devastating indictment from Evan Roberts, who led the 1904 Revival). **P12...£1.20***

A/44   **Is It Wrong to Make These Things Public?** *(Answer to critics). **P8... 80 p.***

A/45   **Unconditional Depends on Conditional**

A/46   Holy Days? Is Christmas evidence of paganism?
A/47   **Is Christmas Truly Pagan?**
A/48   **Self Harm.**
A/49   **What and Where is 'Zion'?**

A/59   Not yet available
A/60   **Can Both Be Spirit-Filled?** *(Charismatics claim equality with others. Is this true?).* **P7...70p**
A/61   **The Hammer of God** *(A dire warning to charismatic leaders from Jeremiah 23).* **P12...£1.20**
A/62(1) **The Alpha Course.** *(A critical analysis of the* **A/62(2)** *main text used for the course).* **Three Articles, 34 A/62(3)** *pages....£3.40 total.*
A/63   **Understanding Regeneration. P6... 60p**
A/64 – A/70   Not yet available
A/71   **True Spirit Behind the TB - A Testimony** *(What ex-Elim leaders say about the TB!).* **P9...90 p**
A/72   **Evangelical Alliance Press Release and BTM Response.** *(The EA misleads churches on TB).* **P8...80 p.**
A/73   **Letters Between BTM & Evangelical Alliance** *(Concerning the TB).* **P9...90 p.**
A/74   **Charismatics & Charismatics** *(Not all are the same. But all are guilty).* **P8...80 p.**
A/75   **A Statement About Livets Ord** *(By the Archbishop of Sweden re Swedish charismatics).* **P2...20 p.**
A/76   **The Problem with Marriage Problems** *(The root cause of marriage problems).* **P9...90 p.**
A/77   **Abuses of Faith** *(Testimonies of two Swedish ex-charismatics).* **P4...40 p.**
A/78   **Apostles** *(Are Apostles with us today? A Biblical examination).* **P5...50 p.**
A/79   **Christian Power** *(Mentioned in scripture - but what is it?).* **P10...£1**
A/80   **The 'Christian Channel'** *(Our objections to this new satellite TV company).* **P8...80 p.**
A/81   **Doctrine** *(What is doctrine?).* **P12...£1.20**

A/82	**Abortion Affects Medical Careers** *(Testimony of how a doctor who refused to perform abortions was penalised).* ***P4...40 p.***
A/83	**New Tribulation for JW's.** *(A new teaching that could split JW'ism down the middle! An exclusive written by an ex-JW leader).* ***P4...40 p.***
A/84	**Why Oppose Charismaticism and the Evangelical Alliance?** *(The Biblical reasoning behind BTM's opposition).* ***P10...£1***
A/85	**What is A Railing Accusation?** *(We are charged with this - so what does the Bible say!).* ***P10...£1***
A/86	**From Faith in Faith to Faith in Christ.** *(Testimony of an ex-'Signs & Wonders' preacher!).* ***P3...30 p.***
A/87	**The 'Word' and the 'word'.** *(God's 'word' does NOT always refer to Jesus Christ!).* ***P6...60 p.***
A/88	**Is There a Special 'Tribulation'?** ***P4...40p.***
A/89	**Election and 'Whosoever'.** *(What scripture says: An important study).* ***P16...£1.60***
A/90	**What is 'Heaven'?** *(A brain-teaser!).* ***P3...18 p.***
A/91	**John Wimber** *(A False Prophet).* ***P6...60 p***
A/92	**William Branham** *(Pentecostalist or Spiritualist?).* ***P6...60 p***
A/93	**The Kansas City Prophets** *(Occultists - NOT true prophets of God).* ***P7...70 p.***
A/94	**Free Will & the Arminian Heresy** *(A theological perspective).* ***P4...40 p***
A/95	**Charismaticism - Satan's Bridge** *(The link between all cults and false religions).* ***P6...60 p***
A/96	**Marc Dupont, John Arnott & Wes Campbell** *(False prophets of charismaticism).* ***P6...60 p***
A/97	**Blotted out of the Book of Life?** ***P5...50 p***
A/98	**A Word to Pastors.** ***P12...£1.20***
A/99	**Response to EMW Concerning Alpha.** (Incomplete)
A/100	**Reformed Brethren?** ***P7...70 p***
A/101	**Mother Theresa -** *Arch Enemy of God.* (Not yet available)
A/102	**Therapeutic Touch** *(Occultism in clinics and hospitals).* ***P8...80p***

A/103   **Pensacola - Deception by Another Name.** *(Another Satanic ploy!).* ***P6...60p***

A/104   **Hypnotism Equals Toronto Blessing/Occultism.** ***P7...70p***

A/105 – A/106   Not yet available

A/107   **Killing & Christian Pacifists.** *Does the Bible REALLY call for pacifism?*

A/110   **Genealogy of Jesus** *(Simple notes based on the genealogy in Matthew One).* ***P4...40p***

A/111 – Not available

A/112   **Benny Hinn & Charismaticism – the Satanic in our Churches.** ***P8…80p***

A/113 -114   Not yet available

A/115   **Azusa Street – the birth of a lie** *(Proof that Pentecostalism and charisaticism are rooted in the occult).* ***P7...70p***

A/116   **Antidote to Reformationism** *(Countering the effects of dead reformationism).* ***P10...£1***

A/117   **The 1997 EA Manifesto – a continuation of folly** *(Evangelical Alliance is an irrelevance in church life).* ***P13...£1.30***

A/118   **About Alpha: January 1999** *(Update).* ***P12...£1.20.***

A/119   Not yet available

A/120   **This is Mine, All Mine!** *(How Christians abuse their income and are worldly).* ***P14...£1.40***

A/121   **As One?** *(A Reformed pastor believes we are 'as one' with charismatics. How wrong he is!).* ***P9...90p***

A/122   **Accepted in the Beloved** *(The love of God toward His own).* ***P8...80p***

A/123   **The Death of Christ – Some pertinent facts.** *(Raw reality & no nonsense)* ***P4...40p***

A/124   **Allowing Sin to Peter Out.** *(Examination of this vital mistake made by reformed men).* ***P6...60p***

A/125   **Letter to Homosexuals from an ex-Homosexual** *(Shows this perversion to be a deliberate choice – a bad habit).* ***P2…20p***

A/126   **Do Babies Automatically go to Heaven?** *(The scriptural answer).* ***P5...50p***

A/127 Can We Prevent Salvation? *(By using hard words).* ***P7...70p***

A/128 Yes, Jesus Did Say He Was God! *P6...60p*

A/129 Violence – a Christian Response. **P8**

A/130 Response to Critics of Article A/01 (Are Prayer Meetings Valid?). ***P16...£1.60***

A/131 Summary of Pentecostalism *(Basic introduction. More to follow).* ***P10...£1***

A/132 and A/133   Not yet available

A/134 'friend of the world' = 'enemy of God'. *(We cannot love the world and claim to be of God).* ***P7...70p***

A/135 Will Christianity Survive? *(An answer to a sceptic).* ***P8...80p***

A/136 Benny Hinn & Charismaticism *(Satanic to the core!).* ***P6...60p***

A/137 Jesus is God. *(A simple statement of fact, yet many Christians show, by their lives and beliefs, that they do not really believe it!).* ***P4...40p***

A/138 Not yet available

A/139 King Saul – Just Like Us! *(Words of warning from the life of this doomed man).* ***P5...50p***

A/140 Look For the Good Points? *(The error of this modern ideology in churches)* ***P4...40p***

A/141 Did God Lie? *(Some say He did...so read this short defence).* ***P4...40p***

A/142 If You Are Living In a Nursing Home, then read this! *(A tough talking Gospel presentation for those who have avoided it all their lives. To be used with discretion). P5...50p*

A/143 Music! Some of the arguments. *(An ongoing article looking at a vexed question. To be updated on occasions)* ***P6...60p***.

A/144 The Jesuit Oath & The Cardinals' Oath. *(Are these authentic oaths showing us the true murderous heart of Rome?)* ***P8...80p***

A/145 Another Jesus, Another Spirit, another Gospel *(Summary of why charismatics must be opposed)* ***P10+...£1***

A/146   **Amateurs Let Loose!** *(Why the 'position' of church counsellors is not required).* ***P6...60p***

A/147   **'Untempered Morter'** *(The case against charismaticism from Ezekiel 13).* ***P6...60p***

A/148   **Human Rights** *(Do we have any?)* ***P7...70p***

A/149   **John 3:16** *(Used by Arminians to prove God offers salvation to everyone – but it does the opposite!)* ***P5...50p***

A/150   **Predestination** *(The Biblical Facts)* ***P4...40p***

A/151   **Justified by Works?** *P5...50p*

A/152   **By Whose Authority?** *(A spirited response to those who reject our ministry)* ***P8...80p***

A/155   **Arminianism and the Doctrines of Grace** *(Basic teaching on TULIP versus Arminianism)* ***P31...£3***

A/156   **Does Free Will Exist?** *(Argument Against Arminianism)* ***P7...70p***

A/157   **Texts Used by Arminians to 'Prove' They Have Free Will** *(Shows their flawed argument)* ***P7...70p***

A/158   **Prayer Meetings... Peter Masters.** He is wrong!

A/161   **Is There a Muslim Threat?**

A/173   **A Kind of Murder** *(Adultery).* **P6...60p**

A/174   **Heresy – from a Heresy's Point of View** *(How Rome sees the Reformation etc).* **P10...£1**

A/175   **How Many Resurrections?** **P4...40p**

A/176   **Peace?** *(promised by God?).* **P5...50p**

A/177   **The UN's One-World Plans.** **P3...30p**

A/178   **Legalising Immorality** *(New laws for Nurses).* **P11...£1.10p**

A/179   **One God, Three Persons.** **P4...40p**

A/180   **Why Rome Objects to the 39 Articles.** **P3...30p**

A/181   **Sin & Sinners** *(Anecdotal).* **P4...40p**

A/182   **Separation Without Cause.** **P5...50p**

A/184   **The Birth of Christ** *(As per scripture).* **P3...30p**

A/188   **Predestination & Election.** **P4...40p**

A/190   **Matthew 16:13-20** *(showing proper Biblical interpretation).* **P5...50p**

A/193   **The Elijah List** *(another charismatic heresy).* **P7...70p**

A/194   **Benny Hinn** *(unfinished).* **P7...70p**

A/195   **Charismatic Scenarios.** **P5...50p**

A/196   **Did God Speak to Arafat?** **P9...90p**

A/198   'The Passion of the Christ' *(Review)*. **P11...£1.10**
A/199   **What is a False Gospel? P8...80p**
A/200   **Homosexuality & the Church. P14...£1.40**
A/201   **Common Grace. P 3...30p**
A/202   **Homosexual Sin in Marriage** *(sad testimony of a wife battered by gay husband)*. **P4...40p**
A/204   **Predestination is a Catholic Dogma** *(taught by Rome, but not scripturally)*. **P4...40p**
A/205   **The Elijah List 2. P5...50p**
A/209   **Our Abilities in Paradise & Heaven. P9... £1**

Thomas Aquinas Series (For a more detailed analysis of his theology see book 'Tom Got it Wrong' – published in early 2007. Details available on my Lulu page):

A/220   **On Predestination, Part 1. P4...40p**
A/221   **As above, Part 2. P3...30p**
A/222   **As above, Part 3. P3...30p**
A/223   **As above, Part 4. P3...30p**
A/224   **As above, Part 5. P7...70p**
A/225   **As above. Part 6. P4...40p**
A/226   **As above, Part 7. P4...40p**
A/227   **As above, Part 8. P4...40p**
A/228   **All of the above, combined. P32...£3.20**

Roman Curia Series *(showing departments in the Vatican. Not yet complete):*

A/230   **Secretariat of State. P4...40p**
A/231   **Congregations. P9...90p**
A/237   **Swiss Guard. P5...50p**
A/252   **Homosexuals are Heterophobic. Review 2005. P30...£3.00**
A/255   **Bullying in the Workplace** *(Case study. Victimisation of Christians in the UK for their beliefs)*. **P10...£1.00 PRIVATE USE ONLY**
A/257   **Adventure in Adversity.** *One woman's fight against the ravages of M.E.* **P6... 60p**
A/258   **Ex-Gay.** Proof that being gay is just a sinful habit and can be stopped. **P4... 40p**
A/261   **The Great Argument (between Wesley and Whitefield). P28... £2.60**
A/262   **Wesley's 'Outward Signs'. P6... 60p**

A/263   **Yes, God Hates!** *But not as we do.* **P4... 40p**

A/265   **Miracles of God, in Our Time.** *A look at the Protestant belief that there are no miracles after the apostles.* **P8... 80p**

A/266   **Marxist Subversion & Perversion of America's Youth. P5... 50p**

A/267   **Hate Crimes & Hate Speech.** Distortion of truth by homosexuals. **P22... £2.20**

A/269   **The Bolsheviks 'Gay Pride' Disaster & Its Lesson for America. P4... 40p**

A/270   **Trotsky's 'Permanent Revolution' in America. P4... 40p**

A/273   **Global Warming.** *A quick examination of these lies put out by governments.* **P10... £1**

A/275   **"Fight the Good Fight"! But How?** Saying it is one thing – living it is quite another! **P23... £2.30**

A/276   **Works (what are they?). P8... 80p**

A/277   **Can America Survive Evolutionary Humanism? P6... 60p**

A/278   Notes on Matthew 5:43-48 (love our enemies?). This is a tough one! P3... 30p

A/279   **Precognition & Retrocognition – Dark Knowledge.** An aspect of modern occultism. **P5... 50p**

A/281   **Dirt-Covered Gold (Our true nature). P4... 40p**

A/283   **Rose's Devotionals.** Anecdotal bio-pics. **P5...50p**

A/284   **Rose's Devotionals.** More bio-pics. **P3... 30p**

A/285   **Rose's Devotionals.** More bio-pics. **P4... 40p**

A/286   **Hell – Rehab or Punishment? P6... 60p**

A/290   **Islam Our Friend?** A response to the Amman Message sent by Islamic leaders to the West. It proves that Islam is not our friend, but must be regarded with suspicion and wariness. **P29...£2.90**

A/291   **Faith: The Reality. P24...£2.40**

A/292   **Does God Answer Prayer? P15... £1.50**

A/293   **The Materialist Faith of Communism, Socialism & Liberalism. P8... 80p**

A/296   **Original Sin. P4... 40p**

A/297   **Where Did Sin Come From? P5... 50p**

A/298   **Death. Then What? P3... 30p**

A/299   **Law and Grace. P8... 80p**

A/300   **Sundays and the Sabbath. P8... 80p**

A/302   Preterism. P6…60p
A/304   MacLeod Controversy Revisited. P22… £2.20
        (Also available as a booklet, publ. Lulu)
A/305   How Do Choices Fit Predestination? P5… 50p
A/306   Philosophy. P6… 60p
A/307   An Arminian Letter. P9… 90p
A/308   Evolution: A Recap. P7… 70p
A/310   What is Hell? *Is it for punishment or purification?* P4…
        40p
A/312   Familism – the Love Syndrome
A/315   Peace With God; How to Achieve it.
A/316   Assurance – How do we get it?
A/317   Was Peter in Rome? Is There Succession?
A/318   Rome and the Bible
A/319   Real Pesence? A Catholic Delusion
A/320   Learning and Stuff. P8… 80p
A/328   Arminianism – Rejects Lead Texts. P*… 80p
        How Arminians are unable to argue logically
A/329   Form Criticism, Intellectual Unbelief. P…4
A/330   Arminianism in Reformed writings. P…3
A/331   New Covenant Theology. P…5
A/332   Why No Christian Can be Green. P…3
A/333   Not yet available
A/334   How to Respond to Unsaved Parents
A/335   Celtic Christianity is not Authentic Christianity
A/336   The Amish
A/337   When God Does not Seem to Answer
A/338   Radical Reformers & Mennonites
A/339   Position Paper: Homosexuality.
A/340   Unitarianism (Also see A/554)
A/341
A/342   Elijah List Issues Fake Obama Prophecy
A/343   not yet available
A/344   The Passover Meal.
A/345   Should Christians Support a Corrupt   Government?
A/346   False ideas on Divorce
A/347
A/348   Biblical Reasons for Divorce
A/349   The Restored Church of God. Is it the true church?

A/350   Satanic Rulers…Obama, Blair, EU & UN
A/351   The World Transformation Movement.
A/352   Self-Creation is Impossible. P8/£80p
A/353   FIRST IN SERIES OF 10 PARTS:
         'Man's Unbelief Shown in Philosophy'.
A/354-on Each part in series looks at specific philosophies that
         affected thinking in each era. Each part is about 10-14
         pages or longer. Ask for list of articles in series.
A/380   Absolute Nothing, Secondary Nothing & Creation.
         P9/£1
A/381   Contextual and Universal Validity. P4/50p
A/382   Forms of Civil Government. P9/£1
A/383   Is Christianity Socialist? P10/£1.10
A/384   The Subtlety of Arminianism. P4/50p
A/385   Ezekiel 28:11-19. Does it use typology or symbolism?
         P12/£1.40
A/386   Geneva's One-Time Glory. P6/70p
A/387   Homosexual Fascism. P5/60p
A/388   Not yet completed
A/389   Was J C Philpot a Mystic Who Taught Pietism? P8/ 90p
A/390   More Arminian Error. P16/£1.80p
A/391   Once Saved, Always Saved
A/392   The King James Bible *(Also see KJAV series)*
A/393   'The Cloud of Unknowing'. Mystic prayer.
A/394   Separation of Church & State (as applied to Registrars).
A/395   Chicago-Lambeth Articles
A/396   Soaking – another charismatic deception P4
A/397   The 95 Theses of Martin Luther. P8
A/398   The Folly of Anthropomorphism (attributing humanity to
         animals)
A/399   BBC2, 'The Bible's Buried Secrets'. Part 3: More
         Nonsense. P10/£1.20
A/400   A Christian Attitude to Homosexuality. P28/£3.
A/401   What the Bible Says about Fools. P7/85p
A/402   Love (Bible Definitions). P6/75p
A/403   God Chooses Who Will be Saved (everything else is a
         lie). P5/65p

A/404	Westcott and Hort (unbelievers who influenced millions). Two unbelieving theologians and their Bible version. **P11/£1.30**
A/405	Character of Joseph Smith, Founder of Mormonism. **P4/55p**
A/406	The Book of Mormon (based on divination). **P5/65p**
A/407	Mormonism. **P18/£2.**
A/408	Youth Are NOT 'Leaving the church'! **P4/55p**
A/409	The Colour of Sound (Art series). **P2/30p**
A/410	Spaces Between Spaces (Art series). **P5/65p**
A/411	Walking and Art (Art series). **P4/55p**
A/412	Agnosticism: the new kid on the block. **P5/65p**
A/413	Wine in Jesus' Time (fermented or unfermented?). **P4/55p**
A/414	Women and Head Covering (1 Cor 11). **P4/55p**
A/415	Divorce and Spouse Abuse. **P12/£140**
A/416	Healing in the New Testament. **P4/55p**
A/417	Homosexuality is a Taboo (with no human rights). **P12/£140**
A/418	
A/419	Quakers (Religious Society of Friends), 2011 Update. **P25/£2.75**
A/420	Homosexuality – a Death Cult. 2011 Update. **P13/£150**
A/421	Do All Scriptural Laws apply to us Today? **P6/75p**
A/422	Claimants to Messiahship *(Jewish, Christian, Islamic and other)*. **P22/£2.50**
A/423	Are We Justified at the Cross or in Eternity? **P3/45p**
A/424	Robert Barnes, First Reformation Preacher in England. **P4/55p**
A/425	Can we Judge Unbelievers? **P5/70p**
A/426	New Calvinism – More charismatic delusion. **P11/£1.35**
A/427	Lectio Divina *More error about prayer*. **P6/75p**
A/428	Are There Two Wills in God? **P30/£3.30**
A/429	McArthur's Millennial Argument.
A/430	The Will of God. **P7/90p**
A/431	Renovare (A cult). **P4/60p**
A/433	New Apostolic Reformation
A/434	Billy Graham – Still Apostate
A/435	'Prophecy of the Popes': Peter the Roman.

A/469   **Augustine and Creation. P10/£1.50.**
A/470   **Invaded by Bad Thoughts? P4/90p.**
A/471   **Did Jesus Know the Time of the Last Day? P5/£1.**
A/472   **Self-Harm. An introduction. P5/£1.**
A/473   **"How should we then live?" P8/£1.30**
A/474   **Origen and New Bible Versions. P3/80p**
A/475   **Tithing. P6/£1.10.** We are not obliged to tithe!
A/476   **Higher Criticism; the evil eye. P15/£2.10** (also listed as KJAV/07)
A/477   **Westcott & Hort, 2. P7/£1.20** (also listed as KJAV/05)
A/478   **Death of a Bible School (The spiritual demise of WEST – Wales Evangelical School of Theology). Part One – Intro. P2/70p.**
A/479   **The Right Direction? Part 2 of the WEST story. P18/£2.30.** Details the reasons for the demise.
A/480   **Wales Evangelical School of Theology – Non-separated and defying God. Part 3. P31/£3.50.**
A/481   **When Error is Made a Virtue (WEST excuses for non-separation). P18/£2.30**
A/482   **Was it "thee days and three nights", or "the third day"? P5/£1.** Looks at the idea that Christ arose NOT on the third day but on the fourth. This idea casts doubt on scripture and forces scripture to contradict itself. It is erroneous.
A/483   **Looking After Someone with Dementia. P11**
A/484
A/485   **Spiritual Warfare. P6/$1.10**
A/486   **The Orality Movement; cultism in disguise. P9/£1.40**
A/487   **Antinomianism** (intro). **P4/90p**
A/488   **Luke 22:19. What is communion supposed to remember? P6/£1.40.** The text is subtle – most Christians miss its true meaning!
A/490
A/491   **The Charge by Atheists, that Christians Use Non-Sequiturs in Argument. P12/£1.70.** Every point is crushed!
A/492   **The Demonic Reality of Charismaticism.**
A/493   **Charismatic Error: the Faith Movement. P11/£1.60**
A/494

A/495   **Non-Sequiturs and Erroneous 'Scriptural' Arguments. (NOT COMPLETED)**

A/496   **The Sin of Sodom. P6/£1.10.** The evil of Sodom was not just homosexuality – it was far more complex and wicked!

A/497   **Giants and Myths. P4/90p.** Yes, there WERE giants!

A/498   **Jesus' Explanation in John 11. P7/£1.20.** Read why Jesus did not hurry to save Lazarus.

A/499   **The Radical Reformation. P8/£1.30.** This is about preachers who broke away from the main reformation groups.

A/500   **Socinianism. P3/80p**

A/501   **Homeostatic Theology. P5/£1.**

A/502   **Welsh outpouring? Genuine or Fake?** The latest example of charismatic fakery. **P11/£1.60**

A/503   **The Jesus of Christianity Compared to the Jesus of Mormonism. P13/£1.80.**

A/504   **Non-Human Personhood...an ungodly fallacy. P4/90p**

A/505   Does God Have Emotions? P9/£1.40

A/506   **The Enneagram: a Satanic Occult Spiritual Tool within the Churches. P3/80p**

A/507   **Charismatics – our view. P5/90p**

A/508   **Faith in the Old Testament (Introductory notes). P3/80p**

A/509   **Acts 8: A Second Blessing of the Holy Spirit? P7/£1.20**

A/510   **Is Sola Scriptura True? (A review of orthodox claims). P30/£3.70.** *Reply to a book by an Orthodox priest denying this vital truth.*

A/511   **Sola Scriptura – an outline. P7/£1.30.** Biblical outline of this truth.

A/512   **Disappearance of Heroes.** *Where are they?* **P4/90p**

A/513   **What makes Christianity True? P7/£1.30**

A/514   **Girls Attracted to 'Bad Boys'. It is not 'love'... Christian girls, beware! P11/£1.60**

A/515   **Is it Rational to believe in God?**

A/516   "When Young Children or the Unborn Die, do they go to Heaven?" A critical appraisal. P9/£1.40

A/517   **Did Darwin repent on His Death Bed? P6/£1.10**

A/518   **Psychiatry – an Overview (Also listed as PSY/08).** *The latest book on the subject – but only repeats much of my own views from the 1970s!*

A/519   **'The Christmas Thing'. Yes to truth, but no to vengeful attitudes.**

A/520   **Red Letter Ministries. The latest charismatic goofery.** *People are still surprised when they come across yet more charismatic trash, But why? Charismaticism has plenty more left in it to shock and dismay! This is because it is of the devil and not of God.*

A/521   **Can Holy Days Be Personal? P4/90p.** *Yes, they can! Scripture says so... but only if the day held to be sacred really is is line with scripture.*

A/522   **Did Jesus die only for the elect, or for everyone? P8/£1.30.**

A/523   **How Gay Propaganda Twists Truth. P8/£1.30.** *We often receive threats and abuse from gays, but this article responds to two ignorant emails from a supposed Christian.*

A/524   **For Whom Did Christ Die? P9/90p** *NOT for 'everybody'!*

A/525   **Plymouth – A Deception Too Far. P8/80p** *(Cultic)*

A/526   **Are Modern 'Tongues' Valid? P4/40p**

A/527   **What Is A Disciple? P5/50p**

A/528   **Frivolous and Veaxtious Litigation (An homosexual/atheist ploy). P6/60p**

A/529   **Total Depravity. P4/90p.** *Written by a deaf pastor to a deaf church. A remarkable understanding of total depravity, when one considers how hard it is for deaf people to learn both written and spoken language.*

A/530   **The Ultimate Conspiracy – Dave Hunt and the Jesuit Attempt to Hijack the Christian Faith. P12/£1.20.**

A/531   **The Sun Stood Still. P4/40p**

A/532   **Calvin and Evangelism. P5/50p**

A/533   **Calvin and Politics. P8/80p**

A/534   **Charismatics Again Vaunting Unbiblical Tongues. P4/40p**

A/535   **Should Christians be Involved with Politics? P5**

A/536   **What is an Arminian? According to John Wesley. P6/£1.10.**

A/537

A/538   **Straight Talk on Homosexuality. P6/60p**

A/539   The Conditions of Omar. Why Muslims are Killing Christians. P7/£1.20.
A/540   ARE we Conquerors? P4/40p
A/541   Grace and Mercy. What do they mean? P8
A/542
A/543   Discrimination – Vital for Right Thinkers. P4
A/544   The House of Hillel, and Paul. P5.
A/545   Holy Spirit – 'it' or 'he'? P5
A/546   When Did Jesus Go Into the Desert? P3
A/547   Jewish Festivals. *(A list)*.
A/548   Predestination and Foreknowledge – not the same.
A/549   Leprosy.
A/550   Jesus, Swords, and Violence
A/551   Jesus in the Old Testament (NOT FINISHED)
A/552
A/553   Filled with the Holy Spirit...How Many Times?
A/554   Unitarian Universalism. *False religion.*
A/555   Amyraldianism. P8. Another error.
A/556
A/557   Did Christ Die for Everyone? *(The Short Answer is – NO!). Read in conjunction with A/555.*
A/558   Amyraldianism 2.
A/559   Are Homosexuals the 'Image of God'? *No!*
A/560   Be Ye Not Unequally Yoked. *God's command usually ignored by many Christians.*
A/561   Purgatory. *Another Catholic Myth.*
A/562   The Authorized Version: its relevance to Christian life and witness today.
A/570   The Waldensians
A/571
A/572
A/573   Confirmation Bias. *A form of sin?* P6
A/574   Self-Defence and Christians. P6. *Important, but will be frowned upon by many!*
A/581   Do Not Help God's Enemies! *Espec. Islamists.*
A/584   The NIV – deceiver of Christians. P14 *(Also listed as KJAV/28*
A/585   Islam Epitomises Marxism. P27
A/586   'Palestine' – the phantom country. P4

A/800 to A/812. Series of articles against homosexuality
originally written for a secular publication. Ask for list
of titles if interested.
(A/2000 Millennium Preaching. P5 *(archive article)*)
A/813   Sodom – a Real Place. P4
A/814   Seal of the Confessional – How Rome hides wickedness.
P10
A/815   Mary – Just a Woman. P10
A/816   Contraception and Christians
A/817   Salvation & Baptism. How they relate to each other. P5
A/818   How to Raise Children (more or less). P4
A/819   Halloween Harms Children. P6
A/820   The 'Day of the Lord'. P4
A/821   Alexander and the Jews. P5
A/822   Jesuits, the Popes, and Islam. P5
A/823   Jesuits and One World Order. (Unfinished)
A/824   Hindu Violence. P3
A/825   Defining the Christmas Argument. P3
A/826   Arab/Muslim Legacy is – Nil. P4
A/827   Prince Charles – Leading Britain into Islam? P7
A/828   Suicide and the Bible.
A/829   Human Philosophy – a paper tiger.
A/830   How Much Does Zero Weigh? P2
A/831   What Does it Say About YOU? (Your attitude towards
Islam and homosexuality).
A/832   Police Attitudes To Islam Wrong. (MPS Twists
language into Nonsense). P12
A/833
A/834   Why God hated the Canaanites.
A/835   The Jewish Temple Existed on Temple Mount. Fact! P6.
A/836   Christians and Violence. A taboo subject. P7
A/837
A/838
A/839   Being Wary of Muslims. P22
A/840   Trust all Muslims? A reasoned Christian Response. P6.
A/841   Jebus/Jerusalem (Both the same). P3.
A/842   Anti-Muslim Bigotry... or biblical reality? P7
A/843   Jerusalem Syndrome. P10.
A/844   Transgender – Stupid Nonsense! P8

A/875   The West Reveres Ramadan – but it is NOT taught by the Koran! P8

A/876   Criticism of Islam. Vital for the whole world and found everywhere. P43

A/877   The British MPs Oath – hypocrisy for status!

A/878   "There be dragons…" *Yes, dragons were real!*

A/879   Steve Chalke – Apostate. P5

A/880   The Police Officer's Oath. P8

A/881   BPD, Grace, Truth & Biblical Boundaries. P3

A/882   God is MALE not Female!

A/883   Jewish Exorcism

A/884   Muslim Immigrants. Are they really saved – or are they playing Christians for fools?

A/885   Deradicalisation is a Secluar Myth. P5

A/886   Genuine Evangelism. P5

A/887   Problem Criticism (of the KJAV). P7

A/888

A/889   Taboos (anatomy and Activity). P14 (vital)

A/890

A/891   Who Gave the Decalogue? God, or Hammurabi? P4 (Also expanded as a book).

A/892   Looking After Someone with Dementia. P4

A/893   The City Falls (How Sweden was destroyed by Muslim migration). P7

A/894   Forced Adoption in the UK. P6

A/895   Chronological Sequence of Resurrection Narrative. P3

A/896   Christ's Resurrection: Commentary on the Texts. P11+ (Now expanded into a book)

A/897   Anxiety, Killer of Life. P5

A/898   Anxiety 2: Response & Warning. P9

A/899   Anxiety 3: chose Sin or Holiness. P8

A/900   Depression: a Dark Reality. P9

A/901   Bunyan on Anxiety and Depression

A/902   Anxiety & Depression: a Testimony. P6

A/903   Is Anxiety or Depression a Sin? P12

A/904   Anxiety & Depression (the Christian Response)

A/905   Neurotic Behaviour 7 What Jesus Said. P2

A/906   Neuroses – Getting Rid of Them. P15

A/907   Christians & Violence. P11.

A/908   **BPD: Not Proved to be Illness. P5.**
A/909   **Keep Breathing.** *(practical health advice)*
A/910   **Hell, Sheol, Hades. P3.**
A/911   **The Steps Leading to breaking God's Taboos.**
A/912   **Christians MUST Speak out.**
A/913   **Jewish Holy Books**
A/914   **Can a Marriage be Voided?**
A/915   **The 'Old Man'.** *Who or what is it?*
A/916   **Paradise & Heaven** . *Seem to be different places*
A/917   **The Pastor Conundrum**. *His real role*
A/918   **Turn the Other Cheek.** *What does it mean?*
A/919   **Scripture & 'Sleep'.** *Not so easy to define.*
A/920   **Comments on Homosexual Advice. 6p**
A/921   **Summary of Facts – Covid19.**
A/922   **'One' or 'One plus One'? (Married or just Together? 9p**
A/923   **View from a Drone, Looking Down.**
A/924   **Bonhoeffer's Theory of Stupidity. 8p**
A/925   **Covid as Mass Hysteria. 11p**
A/926   **Our Righteousness – Filthy Rags. 4p**

<u>Anti-God Beliefs</u>

This series gives a broad outline to false religions, cults, paganisms and occultisms. It will be continued to cover many of these anti-god movements.

AG/00 **Introduction to whole series. P2**
AG/01 **Buddhism. P10**
AG/02 **Hindusim. P14. Satanic to its Core.**
AG/03 **Roman Catholicism. Satan's Masterpiece.**
AG/04 – 1 **Allah. God, or just an idol? P6**
AG/04-2 **What Contemporaries Thought of Islam and Mohammed. P12.** *(not complimentary!)*
AG/05 **Mindfulness-Buddhism. P8**
AG/06 **Seventh Day Adventism**
AG/07 **Islam and Friendships. P11**
AG/08 **Gnosticism**
AG/09 **Christ's Blood & Charismatic Heresy**

<u>Complementary Therapies</u>

These articles vary in length. More added later

CT/01   Acupuncture – Good or Bad? P7/£1.10
CT/02   Aromatherapy. P4/80p
CT/03   Bionenergy. P3/70p
CT/04   Homeopathy. P9/£1.30
CT/05   Indian Head Massage. P4/80p
CT/06   Naturopathy. P10/£1.40
CT/07   Angel Therapy. P
CT/08   Alexander Technique. P
CT/09   Reiki – Occult, not Good P10/$1.40
CT/10   Ex-Reiki (Escaping the Occult). P27/£3.10
CT/11   Body Talk
CT/12   Hopi Ear Candles
CT/13   Kinesiology
CT/14   Psychotherapy
CT/15   Shiatsu
CT/16   Bowen Therapy
CT/17   Hypnotherapy
CT/18   Massage Therapies
CT/19   Reflexology
CT/20   SHEN Therapy
CT/21   Salt Therapies
CT/22   The Enneagram
CT/23   The Kabbalah
CT/24   Magnetic Bracelets (etc).

KJAV & New Versions

This is a series of articles showing the only Bible worth reading is the King James, 1611. It also condemns the new versions for very good reasons. More articles will be added in time. Most, if not all, of these articles will also appear in the general 'Articles' list.

KJAV/Introduction
KJAV/01 Paths of Truth and Error. P10/£1.50
KJAV/02 The New World Bible Version. P4/90p
**KJAV/03 Westcott & Hort (unbelievers who influence
        millions). P10/£1.50**
**KJAV/04 The King James Bible (the finest version ever
        produced). P29/£3.40.**
KJAV/05 Westcott & Hort, 2. P7/£1.20.
KJAV/06 Form Criticism. P4/90p

KJAV/07 Higher Criticism; the evil eye. **P15/£2.10**

KJAV/08 Jesuits, Others, and New Bible Versions (joining the dots). **P27/£3.20.**

KJAV/09 Simple Chronology of KJAV and New   Versions. **P3/80p**

KJAV/10 Examples of New Version Corruption of Truth. **P5/£1.**

KJAV/11 Constantin von Tischendorf – His part in Bible corruption. **P8/£1.30.**

KJAV/12 Behind the Versions. **P10/£1.50.** *(also listed as A/20).

KJAV/13 The Story So Far... **P2/£70p**

KJAV/14 Charismaticism and New Versions. **P8/£1.30.**

KJAV/15 Rome and New Versions. **P4/90p.**

KJAV/16 The Alpha Course and New Versions

KJAV/17 Was It a Camel – or a Rope? Luke 18:25. The story behind this corruption. **P4/90p.**

KJAV/18 New versions. Are they just 'mistaken' or Satanic? **P6/£1.10.**

KJAV/19 New Versions. Can we commend them at all?

KJAV/20 Dunamic Equivalence & the NIV (or 'personalised opinions').

KJAV/AID-1 Paths Taken by KJAV and W&H.

KJAV/21 New King james Version – as bad as the other corrupt versions

KJAV/22 Mary or Miriam? A technical point. **P2/70p**

KJAV/23 NIV – no longer available because it is worthless. **P2/70p**

KJAV/29 Easter – or Passover? Acts 12:4.

KJAV/25 Why Pronouns Must be Correct.

KJAV/26 More on the NIV. **P5**

KJAV-AID-1 Note to understanding

KJAV/27 The AV: Its relevance to today.

KJAV/28 The NIV – deceiver of Christians. **P14**

KJAV/29 Problem Criticism (of KJAV). Also as A/887

Science

A STRAIGHTFORWARD SERIES SHOWING WHAT TRUE SCIENCE REALLY IS and exposing 'science' lies.

Sc/01 **Unscientific Scientists Pretending to do Science. P13/£1.80**

Sc/02 **Can You Believe Evolution and Still be a Christian?** A blunt query that is given a blunt answer!

Sc/03 **Creation Days – Literal, not Poetry. P6/£1.10**

Sc/04 **What is Intelligent Design?**

Sc/05 **The False Gospel of Darwinism. P3/80p**

Sc/06 **Now Camels are Anti-God Missiles!**

Sc/07 **The Sun Stood Still.**

Sc/08

Sc/09 **Bad News for the Big Bang Theory!**

Sc/10 **Infinity – the Never-Ending Story.**

Sc/11 **Dreadnoughtus! Colossal Evidence of Creation and the Flood.**

Sc/12 **Dark Energy. Dark Matter. Unscientific!**

Sc/13 **Ice-Age? The Cold Facts.**

Sc/14 **The Drake Equation (does not equate). P5**

Sc/15 **We are different From Animals After all!**

Sc/16 **Ice Ages? A differing Creationist view. P3**

Sc/17 **Burned Mystery Scroll Digitally Unravelled, Reveals Bible Unchanged for 2000 Years.**

Sc/18` **Christianity stands or falls on the historical accuracy of Genesis.**

Sc/19 **Flagellar Motors, proof of God's design.**

Sc/20 **Carbon Dating, creating false history**

Sc/21 **Cannabis & CBC**

CHRISTIANS & PSYCHIATRY

In this series we look at psychiatry in the widest terms, in the light of scripture. The writer is a qualified psychiatric nurse, has a Master's degree in psychology, and was Clinical Nurse Manager of an Elderly Mentally Frail (EMI/dementia) Unit.

PSY/01 **The Psychiatric World** *(First Article in the 'Christians and Psychiatry' series).* ***P8...80 p.***

PSY/02 **Neuroses** *('breakdowns' or 'nerves').* ***P4...40p***

PSY/04 **Borderline Personality Disorder** *(Said to be the major cause of mental hospital intake – affects young people). P16...£1.60p*

PSY/05 Depression. P7/80p

PSY/06 Talking Therapies – *Godless theories and Counselling.* P7/80p

PSY/07 Borderline Personality Disorder. Reply to critics. P18/£2.30

PSY/08 Psychiatry – a 2013 Overview.

PSY/09 Is Mental Illness 'Biblical'? P8/£1.40.

PSY/10 The M'Naghten Rules. (Bad theory!).

PSY/11 Compulsive Obsessional Disorder. Real Illness – or Imagined? P8

PSY/12 Psychoticism. Real or Invented? P5

PSY/13 The 'Trans' Idiocy.

PSY/14

PSY/15 Anxiety, Killer of Life (also as A/897)

PSY/16 Anxiety 2, Response & Warning (also as A/898)

Psy/17

Psy/18 Depression: a dark reality. P9

Psy/19 Bunyan on Anxiety & Depression.

Psy/20 Anxiety & Depression: a Testimony. P6

Psy/21 Is Anxiety & Depression a Sin? P13.

Psy/22 Anxiety & Depression. The Christian Response.

Psy/23 Neuroses. Getting rid of them.

Psy/24 Schizophrenia. P9

Psy/25 Bi-Polar (Manic Depression).

Psy/26 Using Food to improve Mood (summary only).

Psy/26a Using Food to Improve Mood. P27.

Psy/27 Tourette's Syndrome. (*genuine or fake?*)

Psy/28 Depression & Everybody

Psy/29 OCD – An Emotional Chameleon. 8p

Psy/30 Covid – Marxist/Fascist Weapon of Choice. 10p

Psy/31 Conversion Therapy & Homosexual Illogic

<u>Bible Studies</u>

A new Bible study is published every Sunday.

We go through whole books, showing biblical interpretations and teachings. Only available by email each Sunday. Or, you can order whole books by email, at basic cost. When sent by email they arrive as Word documents. Some books are also published as books by Amazon, Lulu, etc. For a list of these go to the website address shown below. Whole Bible Books completed thus far include:

<u>New Testament</u>
All NT books have been completed, chapter by chapter.
<u>Old Testament</u>
The following have been completed thus far:
1 & 2 Samuel
Daniel
Exodus
Genesis
Haggai
Jonah
Joshua
Judges
Malachi
Obadiah
Psalms (Up to Psalm 113: to be continued)
The Proverbs
1 Kings
2 Kings
Deuteronomy
Job (Extended version published as Bible commentary)
NT and/or OT book studies are added to weekly.
<u>Bible Places</u>
These are provided as a brief aid. They describe places found in scripture and show how they relate to the Bible accounts. They are not reference-numbered because they are being published in alphabetical order. The following are currently available:

A Short Introduction to Bible Places
Accho
Aceldama
Adullam
Ai
Alexandria
Anathoth
Antioch
Antipatris
Arabah
Ashkelon
Asshur
Athens
Jericho
Others will be added as time permits

The Beacon

The Beacon is a monthly newsletter with news and views, sent out by email or by post, to subscribers. Either apply via the website, or email, or when asked to resubscribe annually.

Sunday Studies

These are sent out by email-only every Sunday to those who subscribe to the Sunday list. Each study looks at a Bible book with consecutive chapters, basing interpretation on Hebrew and Greek wordage (or Aramaic, as with Daniel), but presented in ordinary language. There are no denominational or other partisan approaches used in these studies... they only teach what scripture (God) says.

New Articles List

Subscribers to this list receive all new articles 'hot off the press' by email (not by mail). This is because we are still transferring material from our old archive site (www.christiandoctrine.net) and so new articles can take months to appear on the new website. Each month, too, new titles are listed in The Beacon newsletter

General News

Links sent out daily for news and views items. Can be up to two dozen a day. These tend to be important for fellow believers. Just delete anything not of interest!

GENERAL NOTE:

We have other publications that do not appear in this publications list.

There are also books (available either from Lulu or Amazon & bookshops). For list of these go to

http://lulu.com/spotlight/kbnapier

Costs: We pay for all ministry costs ourselves. As K B Napier is now retired (since being forced out of his job by homosexual activists in 2005), this cost is high and gifts to him personally are always appreciated. These are usually diverted to the ministry when required anyway, to add to his own pension contributions.

Most of our work is done by website or email. Costs of postage to both the UK and other countries are additional.

PUBLICATIONS' LIST

This is updated every time we add a new article, so can sometimes change quickly every month.

Note: Every year, around the world, academic seminars and conferences (a few dozen annually) mention works by K B Napier – some approvingly, and some against! And many of our regular readers are pastors/theologians, who appreciate the fact that we do not compromise and we use straightforward language.

Bible Theology Ministries
(BTM: Established 1985)

For details by internet/contact the author:

www.christiandoctrine.com

The above website is the internet presence of BTM.

BTM has several free email lists for subscribers. To be added to one or all of them go to the website.

For full details of up-to-date publications (several thousands) make a request via the website. (The website does not carry all publications yet)

For details of other books by Dr K B Napier, go to website and click on 'books'. Books are distributed by Amazon, bookshops, and by Lulu Publishing. Or, go to:

http://lulu.com/spotlight/kbnapier

To receive details by ordinary mail send to:

BTM, PO Box 415, Swansea, SA5 8YH   UK

BTM/christiandoctrine.com and the co-founders are unpaid. All materials are free if using email. We will make a very small charge to cover postage and paper etc., for items sent by mail.